Design

King George V in 1941, showing her prominent external degaussing coil—the only ship of the class to have this feature. The censor has busied himself with this photograph: something has been deleted from the background, aft of the ship.

THE five battleships of the *King George V* class were the most modern to serve the Royal Navy during the Second World War, and all rendered invaluable service in the promotion of the war effort. The first two ships, in particular, can be credited with influencing the course of the war: they were instrumental in the sinking of the battleship *Bismarck*, the strategic result of which was a fundamental shift in German naval policy involving the promotion of the U-boat arm at the expense of heavy surface ships. This is not, of course, to claim that they directly brought about the Allied victory; but by their action they fundamentally changed the policy of the *Kriegsmarine*, confirming the final burial of the 'Z-Plan' programme of German naval construction which had been killed off shortly after war broke out in favour of further U-boat building.

The design origins of the class lie in the Washington Treaty of 1922,

which stipulated that future capital ships should displace no more than 35,000 tons and be armed with gun calibres no greater than 16in, and to which Britain, the United States, Japan, France and Italy were signatories—limitations which were carried through at the London Naval Conference of 1930, which also confirmed that no new battleships would be laid down until 1937 at the earliest. However, neither France nor Italy signed up, and the news that both countries were laying down new battleship construction with individual vessels built up to the Washington Treaty limits brought about a realisation in Britain that a response of comparable fighting strength was required.

Warship design is an evolutionary process, and it never ceases, even though no hardware may be in immediate prospect, and during the late 1920s and early 1930s British naval architects prepared a number of studies and sketch designs. There was no desire to evolve the *Nelson* class battleships: this pair had been designed to sail at the standard battlefleet speed and shipped the heaviest guns and armour possible, and the new French capital ships—*Dunkerque* and *Strasbourg*—emphasised speed at the cost of firepower. A large number of studies were completed, four of which are shown in the table opposite; the last entry, '14P', would become the final design for the *King George V*s.

↑↑*Prince of Wales* in early 1941. Other than the absence of a degaussing cable, a feature distinguishing her from *King George V* was the provision of only three UP mountings, that on the quarterdeck being replaced by a 40mm Bofors gun—a considerably more useful weapon. The paintwork appears to be in the process of renewal: as with *King George V*, the original coating has taken something of a battering.
↑ The final ship of the class, *Howe*, as completed, late summer 1942.

→→ *King George V* on 9 December 1943, just before paying off to undergo a major refit. She retains the camouflage paintwork first applied in summer 1942.

Armament

From these it can be seen that the Board of Admiralty leant in favour of strong armour protection at the cost of armament calibre and a small sacrifice in speed. The projectile for the 14in gun, at under 1,600lb, compared very unfavourably with that for the standard 15in (1,920lb) and 16in gun (2,050lb) which equipped the Royal Navy's existing capital ships; thus a 1in (6.5 per cent) decrease in calibre resulted in a 16 per cent, not a 6.5 per cent, reduction in shell weight. However, the rate of fire of the 14in gun, at supposedly two rounds per minute, was a big improvement compared with that of 15in and 16in-gunned battleships. The table also shows that twelve 14in guns were originally envisaged, in three quadruple turrets, but before the design was finally closed it was decided to sacrifice two barrels and mount a 14in twin in 'B' position instead of a quadruple so as to allow for thicker armour. The layout of the main armament was still, however, unique for a capital ship.

The secondary armament was also of a new design. The calibre selected, 5.25in, was deemed sufficiently heavy to deal with attacks by destroyer-type vessels and at the same time serve as an effective heavy anti-aircraft gun. The lightly armoured turrets were disposed symmetrically abreast each of the two funnels, in superfiring positions. The barrels could elevate individually up to 80°.

The anti-aircraft armament was originally to comprise four 8-barrelled 2pdr 'pom-poms', later upgraded to

King George V Class: Selected Preliminary Designs, 1934–37

Design	Std displacement (tons)	Length (pp) (ft-in)	Armament	Armour (belt) (in)	shp	Speed (kt)
12N	28,500	570	8 x 12in	12½	45,000	23
16A	35,000	730	9 x 16in	12	112,000	30
14L	35,000	700	12 x 14in	14	100,000	28
14P	35,000	700	10 x 14in	15	100,000	28.5

six, but owing to availability the first two ships were completed with only four mountings. Supplementary AA weapons were added piecemeal as the war progressed, beginning with the infamous and totally impractical UP (Unrotating, or Unrifled, Projectile) mounting, several of which were aboard the first two ships when they commissioned.

Protection

The scale of protection afforded the *King George V* class battleships was in keeping with contemporary thinking, with a greater emphasis on horizontal armour than had hitherto been the case, with the exception of the preceding *Nelson*s. The armour belt, which extended from forward of 'A' turret to just abaft 'Y' turret, was 15in thick at its maximum and 23ft deep, 13ft of which was above the waterline at mean draught. Horizontal armour at main deck level was 6in over the magazines and 5in over the machinery. The whole scheme formed a citadel closed by 12in forward and 10in after bulkheads, expected, generally speaking, to be proof against a 1,000lb bomb dropped from 10,000ft and a plunging 15in shell fired at a range of 30,000yds.

The heavily armoured, separate conning tower, so much a feature of British capital ships even up to the *Nelson*s, was dispensed with in favour of a much more lightly armoured component (4½in–2in) integral with the bridge, and this saved several hundred tons. The main turrets were given 13in faces and 9in–7in sides, with 6in roofs and 7in rears, and there was, as to be expected, a comprehensive scheme of armoured bulkheads and splinter protection. Protection for the secondary armament consisted of 1½in on the front faces and 1in elsewhere.

The anti-torpedo protection involved a novel arrangement based on that adopted for the *Nelson*s, with a 'sandwich' comprising three compart-

↓ The third ship of the class, *Duke of York*, photographed on 3 November 1941. She may be in overall grey finish, although there is a hint of the earlier camouflage scheme around the bows.

King George V Class

	Builder	Laid down	Launched	Completed
King George V	Vickers-Armstrong, Tyneside	1 Jan 1937	21 Feb 1939	11 Dec 1940
Prince of Wales	Cammell Laird, Birkenhead	1 Jan 1937	3 May 1939	31 Mar 1941
Duke of York	John Brown, Clydeside	5 May 1937	28 Feb 1940	4 Nov 1941
Anson	Swan Hunter, Tyneside	20 Jul 1937	24 Feb 1940	22 Jun 1942
Howe	Fairfield, Clydeside	1 Jun 1937	9 Apr 1940	29 Aug 1942

ments, the central space carrying oil fuel (automatically displaced by sea water as it was consumed) and the outer spaces being left void. These special compartments extended the length of the citadel. A 5ft deep double bottom, filled with oil or water, provided additional protection.

Machinery

The basic machinery comprised four sets of Parsons geared turbines fed by eight Admiralty small-tube boilers, two of the latter linked to each turbine, which in turn drove one shaft independently, although boiler output could if necessary be diverted to alternative turbines. The ships' bunker capacity was 3,300 tons of fuel oil.

Electric current was generated by means of two diesel and six turbine-driven 350kW dynamos, with additional auxiliary plant to provide current for harbour duties.

Fire Control

The main armament was controlled via two director control towers, one on top of the bridge superstructure and one abaft the mainmast, each equipped

Prince of Wales on 23 October 1941, now in camouflage. Unfortunately, this complex scheme did nothing to prevent her loss in December 1941 at the hands of Japanese bombers and torpedo aircraft.

with 15ft rangefinders. For local control (in the event that the DCTs were damaged in action), 'A' and 'Y' turrets had integral 41ft rangefinders and 'B' turret a 30ft rangefinder. The 5.25in dual-purpose armament was controlled by four separate DCTs, a pair forward atop the bridge superstructure and a pair aft, abreast the mainmast. Six (originally four) Mk IV 'pom-pom' directors controlled the 2pdr AA guns, five on the bridge structure (two each side abreast and below the HACS director tower and one on the centreline, between the two HACS themselves) and one on the after superstructure.

Radar equipment varied as the five ships entered commission at different stages of technical development. *King George V* and *Prince of Wales* originally had Types 279 air warning/ranging and 284 gunnery radar, aerials for the former atop the fore topmast and for the latter on the main armament director control towers. As the war went on, the ships' radar suites were upgraded as refined technology found its way from drawing board to practical application.

General

The *King George V*s were products of the largest battleship building programme in Britain since the First World War, all five vessels being laid down within a period of seven months. Apart from the one-off *Vanguard*, they were the last British battleships to be built; all gave excellent service, and the four survivors were not disposed of until the late 1950s.

Their main armament proved temperamental and troublesome, prone to mechanical failure, especially during the loading cycle (three years after the first of the class entered service, *Duke of York* was still having trouble at the Battle of the North Cape in her engagement with *Scharnhorst*); the 5.25in secondary battery proved disappointingly slow in its rate of fire; the ships were wet forward owing to the requirement that 'A' turret be able to fire ahead at low elevation (the problem did not ease with the inevitable rise in displacements as extra weight was taken on board during the war); and, as noted earlier, range was disappointingly below par for ships of their type. But their contribution to the war effort was incalculable, especially in terms of their effect on German surface operations and hence their role in safeguarding the vital convoys.

King George V: Outline Legend, 1940

Displacement:	36,727 tons standard, 42,076 tons deep
Dimensions:	Length 745ft overall, 700ft between perpendiculars; beam 103ft; mean draught 29ft standard, 32ft 6in deep
Armament:	10 x 14in Mk VII (2 x 4, 1 x 2); 16 x 5.25in Mk I (8 x 2); 32 x 2pdr (4 x 8); 80 x UP (4 x 20)
Machinery:	Four Parsons geared turbines, eight Admiralty 3-drum boilers; 4 shafts; 110,000shp
Speed:	28kt
Range:	3,100nm at 27kt, 5,750nm at 20kt, 14,500nm at 10kt*

* These design figures were never achieved owing to unexpected steam leakage on the cruising turbine, and in practice the figures were 2,500nm at 27kt and 4,100nm at 20kt. The machinery also required heavy maintenance.

Careers

WITH the declaration of war on 1 September 1939 came the impetus to speed completion of the two new British battleships recently launched, *King George V* and *Prince of Wales*, an impetus given even more urgency with the impending commissioning of *Bismarck* and *Tirpitz*, the two huge capital ships being completed in Germany. Put simply, the Royal Navy had in service little which compared to these new German battleships: those sufficiently armed and armoured to withstand their firepower were far too slow to catch them, and of those big-gun ships fleet enough to be able to bring them to action—the three battlecruisers *Hood*, *Repulse* and *Renown*—only the as yet unmodernised *Hood* was considered to be sufficiently well armoured to be able to counter them. All this would change with the introduction to service of the '*KGV*s'.

KING GEORGE V

The first of the class to be completed, *King George V* was commissioned at her shipyard and sailed for Rosyth on 16 October 1940, there to be ammunitioned and begin her trials. By the end of the year she had joined the Home Fleet at Scapa Flow.

She crossed the Atlantic early in 1941 to take Lord Halifax, would-be Prime Minister of Great Britain but now Ambassador to the United States, to Annapolis and covered an eastbound convoy on her return, arriving back at Scapa on 6 February. Her next task was to provide distant cover for Operation 'Claymore', a Royal Marines raid on the Lofoten Islands off the north-west coast of Norway. Further Atlantic convoys, HX.114 and HX.115, were escorted during March, when the German battleships *Scharnhorst* and *Gneisenau* and the pocket-battleship *Admiral Scheer*—and, it was later discovered, the heavy cruiser *Admiral*

➡➡ *King George V* in dry dock at Rosyth. The paintwork on the lower hull is well battered, although the draught marks—one foot apart and in white-painted roman numerals—seem pristine enough.

Hipper—were at large, but although *King George V* was detached to follow up reports of the German raiders' presence, no engagement resulted.

The *Bismarck* Episode

On 1 April 1941 *King George V* became flagship of the Home Fleet (C-in-C Admiral Sir John Tovey). The first major engagement of her career came along some eight weeks later when, following the loss of *Hood* and the damaging of *Prince of Wales* at the hands of *Bismarck* in the Denmark Strait on 24 May, she and the 16in-gun battleship *Rodney* sighted the wounded German giant after she had been rediscovered and a successful strike had been carried out by Swordfish torpedo-bombers from the aircraft carrier *Ark Royal*.

At 0842 on Tuesday 27 May the enemy came into view. The two British battleships were approaching their quarry head on, in order to close the range as swiftly as possible, and discovered to their surprise that *Bismarck* was doing the same—though helplessly, unmanoeuvrable as she was on account of a torpedo hit from one of the Swordfish. Fire was opened by *Rodney* at 0847; the flagship joined the action less than a minute later, her Type 284 radar providing ranging data, which proved to be little more than 20,000yds. Minutes later *King George V* obtained the first hit, when a 14in shell penetrated the base of *Bismarck*'s forward superstructure.

Following changes of course to bring them steaming parallel, though in the opposite direction, to the enemy, both British battleships resumed fire, and at 0902 a hit from *Rodney* put *Bismarck*'s forward 38cm turrets out of commission; at 0915 a 14in shell from the flagship accounted for 'Dora' turret (i.e., 'Y' turret). By this time the range was down to about 10,000yds, and for the next five minutes 14in and 5.25in shells struck *Bismarck* on several occasions before problems with the loading mechanism in the main turrets meant that thereafter fire was erratic (though nonetheless quite effective).

By 1015 the range was down to less than 3,000yds and *Bismarck* had been hammered into a silent, blazing hulk, her superstructure wrecked beyond recognition and her hull settling in the water, clearly in a sinking condition. Short of fuel, Tovey ordered his battleships to turn for home, leaving other vessels nearby to move in with torpedoes. Within half an hour the German battleship had disappeared beneath the Atlantic waves, but it had taken, probably, some 400 hits by medium- and heavy-calibre shells, not to speak of several torpedoes, to bring about this result.

↓ *King George V* in 1941, in overall grey finish as was standard for capital ships of the Home Fleet at that time.

Watching the Enemy

For the next few months *King George V* remained in home waters, ready to counter any threatening movement by German heavy warships. In November 1941 she sailed to a position south of Iceland following reports that a breakout would soon be attempted by either *Tirpitz* or *Admiral Scheer*. In February 1942 a sortie by *Admiral Scheer* and the heavy cruiser *Prinz Eugen*, escorted by destroyers, to take up new positions in Norwegian fjords took *King George V* north in an attempt to intercept the squadron, but no contact was made; and in March a movement from her anchorage by *Tirpitz* brought a similar response, with, again, no result.

Distant cover for Arctic convoys began in April, and on 1 May, while east of Iceland, *King George V* was involved in a major collision with the destroyer *Punjabi*. The latter was sliced in two and sank, but her exploding depth charges ripped a 30ft gash in the flagship's bows and caused serious power failures. After temporary repairs had been carried out in Iceland, *King George V* was taken into Gladstone Dock in Liverpool, remaining there for two months while the damage was put right.

Convoy operations resumed in December 1942, but *King George V* was still at Scapa, too distant to intervene, when the German Operation 'Regenbogen' got under way on the 31st of the month, though fortunately the attacks on convoy JW.51B, by forces including *Lützow* (ex *Deutschland*) and *Admiral Hipper*, were thwarted by the British close escort and the convoy reached its destination unscathed.

The Mediterranean

In May 1943 *King George V* was moved to Gibraltar preparatory to Operation 'Husky', the Allied invasion of Sicily. She, with sister-ship *Howe*, was allocated to the reserve covering group when the operation got under way on 1 July, a task they fulfilled also for the landings at Salerno (Operation 'Avalanche') which began on 9 September. Some action was seen: the two ships

◆ September 1949: *King George V* with paying-off pendant evident. The ship would see no further active service.

bombarded Trapani in Sicily on 12 July and helped beat off a bombing raid whilst at Algiers prior to departing for 'Avalanche'.

King George V also escorted parts of the Italian Fleet, including the battleships *Andrea Doria* and *Caio Duilio*, to Malta after the Italian armistice, and, with *Howe*, provided cover for the British airborne landings at Taranto from 9 to 11 September. At the end of October, the two sister-ships returned to home waters, *King George V* paying off for refit early in the New Year.

British Pacific Fleet

Prime Minister Churchill's desire for a strong Royal Navy presence in the Pacific sphere of operations led to the formation, in late 1944, of the British Pacific Fleet—somewhat, it has to be said, against the Americans' better judgement—and on 28 October *King George V* sailed from Scapa Flow to join other naval units assembling at Trincomalee, Ceylon.

A stop at Alexandria en route enabled the ship to divert to Milos in the Aegean Sea to bombard German positions there, and on 1 December she resumed her eastward journey, arriving in Trincomalee two weeks later. Operation 'Meridian', the transfer to the Pacific proper, got under way on 16 January 1945. The force, known as Task Force 63, comprised *King George V*, the aircraft carriers *Illustrious*, *Indomitable*, *Indefatigable* and *Victorious*, four cruisers and ten destroyers.

The first stage was an 11,000nm voyage to Sydney, and en route the force attacked oil refineries on Sumatra, practised replenishment-at-sea and beat off a Japanese air attack, *King George V*'s AA crews downing one Mitsubishi Ki-21.

Joined by *Howe* and redesignated TF.57, the BPF made its mark again in late March when it launched attacks on the Sakishimo-Gunto airfields, a sortie it repeated in early May. As the Allies moved in on the Japanese homeland, *King George V* was detached in mid-July to join battleships of the US Navy in a bombardment of industrial installations at Hitachi, north-east of Tokyo, where 267 rounds of 14in were expended. The task force moved on to Hamamatsu in southern Honshu, where it carried out a further bombardment of aviation factories in the locality.

With the dropping of the atomic bombs on Hiroshima and Nagasaki and the immediate Japanese surrender, *King George V* moved with other units of the BPF into Sagami Bay to be present at the surrender ceremonies.

The ship did not return to Britain until March 1946, having been absent for sixteen months and having steamed nearly 75,000nm during that period. Her active career in the Royal

Navy was terminated in June 1950 when she and her sister-ships went into reserve and were 'mothballed'. *King George V* was the first large warship to be preserved in this fashion, which involved sealing the armament, machinery and boilers against damp and installing dehumidifiers throughout the ship.

In 1957 the decision was taken to scrap the four ships, and the following year *King George V* was moved from her berth in the Gareloch to the shipbreaking firm of Arnott Young in Dalmuir to undergo dismantling.

PRINCE OF WALES

The second ship of the class to commission, *Prince of Wales* had arguably the most dramatic, and certainly the shortest, career of the five ships. She famously took part in the *Bismarck* action; was much photographed during her sojourn in Placentia Bay, Newfoundland, having taken Prime Minister Chuchill to his first meeting with President Roosevelt, the result of which was the celebrated Atlantic Charter; and fell victim to aerial bombs and torpedoes off Malaya following a widely criticised decision to send a naval force to demonstrate against the Japanese, and in so doing became the first battleship to be sunk by air attack while under way.

In the Denmark Strait

On 24 May 1941, with confirmation that *Bismarck* was lying in a Norwegian fjord and might be attempting a break-out into the Atlantic at any time, Tovey, C-in-C Home Fleet, began to plan the disposition of his forces to meet the threat. *Hood* and *Prince of Wales*—forming the somewhat incongruously termed 'Battle Cruiser Squadron'—left Scapa Flow at around midnight to take up station south of Iceland, with a view to intercepting the German battleship should she attempt a passage south in that area.

Despite the assurances given by her Captain, John Leach, that his ship was ready for service, this was plainly not the case: full-power trials had been complete only two weeks previously, and the ship sailed with civilian technicians on board still trying to iron out serious problems with the functioning of the main armament.

It is not intended here to give a blow-by-blow account of the battle in the Denmark Strait which ensued when, in the early morning of 24 May, *Hood* and *Prince of Wales* encountered *Bismarck* and her consort, the heavy cruiser *Prinz Eugen* and resulted in the loss of the British flagship; this is a story that has been dealt with in considerable detail in other publications. As far as *Prince of Wales* is concerned, however, the shooting was hampered first by the drenching spray which cascaded over the foreship, blinding the rangefinders as the ship closed the target, and then by mechanical problems in the main turrets, which began to show themselves almost as soon as action was joined. Her sixth salvo straddled *Bismarck*, as did the ninth. It was just after the tenth had been fired that *Hood* perished, following which *Prince of Wales* received the undivided attention of the German ships, and over the next ten minutes she received seven hits, three of which detonated. One passed through the compass platform without exploding but killed everyone in the vicinity except Leach and two of his officers; one entered the ship below the waterline but did not explode; and another exploded aft, within the hull. The latter two caused the ingress of some 600 tons of sea water, but the fighting efficiency of the ship was unimpeded. Leach decided to break off the action, 'pending a more favourable opportunity.'

Much has been written about the supremacy of the two German ships in this action, and how they managed to sink *Hood* and force *Prince of Wales* to retire. In truth, the British battleship won the engagement, however unfashionable it may be to say so. She struck *Bismarck* three times—*Bis-*

marck scored the same number of hits on her—the most damaging involving a shell which ruptured two oil tanks forward, severed their links to the boilers, caused *Bismarck* to take aboard 2,000 tons of sea water and compelled the German admiral, Lütjens, to sail to France for repairs, his ship well down by the bow. This damage was the catalyst that enabled *Bismarck* to be brought to battle by other units of the Home Fleet, wherein she perished.

Prince of Wales re-engaged *Bismarck* later on 24 May, firing twelve salvos without result and experiencing further mechanical problems; and two more salvos were managed just after midnight on 25 May. At 2000 that day she withdrew to Iceland to refuel.

Summit Meeting

Following repairs at Rosyth and a period of working-up, *Prince of Wales* took Churchill across the Atlantic for a conference with US President Roosevelt. She arrived in Placentia Bay, Newfoundland, on Saturday morning, 9 August 1941, and following much ceremony culminating in the signing of the famous Atlantic Charter, the ship returned home, via Iceland, arriving at Scapa on 18 August.

The following month she was assigned to Force H, in the Mediterranean, and took the opportunity of escorting a Malta convoy on the way south (Operation 'Halberd'). On 27 September the convoy was attacked by Italian aircraft, and later that day there were reports that units of the Italian Fleet were approaching. *Prince of Wales*, the battleship *Rodney* and the carrier *Ark Royal* were despatched to intercept, but the search proved fruitless. The convoy safely delivered, *Prince of Wales* returned to Gibraltar and then to Scapa, arriving there on 6 October.

Demise

Churchill's insistence that a Royal Navy presence in Far Eastern waters be established in order to demonstrate his determination to foil Japanese deisgns in that region—reinforced by his 'Action This Day' minute to the Admiralty—saw *Prince of Wales* and a destroyer escort leave home waters on 25 October bound for Singapore, there to meet up with the battlecruiser *Repulse* and the carrier *Indomitable*. The last, however, ran aground off Jamaica a few days later and was unable to proceed.

Calling at Freetown and Cape Town to refuel (and to generate publicity), and again at Mauritius and the Maldive Islands, *Prince of Wales* reached Colombo, Ceylon, on 28 November, joining up with *Repulse* the next day. On 2 December the fleet docked in Singapore.

Japanese troop convoys were sighted as quickly as 6 December, and on the 8th—the day after the Pearl Harbor attack—Singapore was raided by Japanese aircraft, in response to which *Prince of Wales*'s anti-aircraft batteries opened up, albeit without effect. A signal was received from the Admiralty in London ordering the British squadron to commence hostilities, and that evening, confident that a protective air umbrella would be pro-

↑ *Prince of Wales* in Placentia Bay, Newfoundland, having conveyed Prime Minister Churchill across the Atlantic for the meeing with US President Roosevelt which would result in the signing of the Atlantic Charter. The ship alongside is the destroyer *McDougal* (DD 358), which brought the President to the battleship for the conference.

Prince of Wales on 6 October 1941, still in camouflage but with a white top to her after funnel.

vided by the RAF presence in the region, Admiral Phillips set sail.

Force Z, as it was dubbed, comprised *Prince of Wales* and *Repulse*, plus the destroyers *Electra, Express, Vampire* and *Tenedos*. The object of the sortie was to attack Japanese transports at Kota Bharu, but in the afternoon of 9 December a Japanese submarine spotted the British ships, and in the evening Japanese aerial reconnaissance located them. By this time it had been made clear that no RAF fighter support would be forthcoming. Then, at midnight, a signal was received that Japanese forces were landing at Kuantyan in Malaya. Force Z was diverted to investigate. At 0211 on the 10th the Force was sighted again by submarine, and at 0800 it arrived off Kuantan, only to discover that the reported landings were a fiction.

At 1100 that morning the first Japanese air attack got under way. Eight Type 96 'Nell' bombers deposited their bombs close to *Repulse*, one passing through the hangar roof and exploding on the 1in plating of the main deck below. The second attack arrived at 1130, and comprised seventeen 'Nells' armed with torpedoes, divided into two attack formations. *Prince of Wales* was struck twice, although *Repulse* managed to dodge the seven torpedoes aimed at her, as she did the bombs dropped minutes later by a further formation of six 'Nells'.

The torpedoes which struck the *Prince of Wales*, on the port side, wrecked the outer propeller shaft on that side and put the entire electrical system in the after part of the ship out of action. Unable to combat the problems with effective damage control, she immediately took on a heavy list. She was, in reality, finished.

A third torpedo attack developed against *Repulse*, and once again she succeeded in avoiding any strikes, but a fourth attack, by torpedo-carrying Type 1 'Bettys', sank her at 1233. Six aircraft from this attack made for *Prince of Wales*, and four torpedoes hit the ship, causing further damage and flooding. Finally, a 500kg bomb planted squarely on the catapult deck penetrated through to the main deck and exploded there, tearing a gash in the port side of the hull and admitting still further sea water. At 1315 the order to abandon ship was given, and at 1320 the battleship went under, her Admiral and Captain among the 327 fatalities.

DUKE OF YORK

It was ironic that *Prince of Wales* was lost just five weeks after her newest sister-ship, *Duke of York*, was completed; and ironic, too, that the new ship's first duty was to take the Prime Minister across the Atlantic once more, this time to attend the 'Arcadia' conference. She left the Clyde on 13 December and arrived at Norfolk, Virginia nine days later after gales and detours to avoid U-boats had caused delays. The ship returned to Scapa on 21 January 1942, Churchill having decided to fly home in order to save time.

On Watch

Anxiety concerning *Tirpitz* saw *Duke of York* despatched to Iceland at the end of January to help guard against a break-out by the German battleship, and by March she was providing distant cover for the Arctic convoys between Iceland and Norway, in which role she continued until October, without serious incident. She became the flagship of the Home Fleet during *King George V*'s enforced absence through June and July to undergo repairs following her collision with the destroyer *Punjabi*.

'Torch', 'Camera', 'Husky'

The Allied invasion of North Africa saw *Duke of York* sailing south to the Mediterranean to reinforce Force H in late October. Air attacks developed, but these were relatively puny and swiftly dealt with the 'umbrella' provided by the aircraft from the accompanying carriers *Victorious*, *Formidable* and *Furious*. Mission accomplished, the ship returned to Britain for refit.

Duke of York resumed her status as flagship from 14 May 1943 pending the departure of *King George V* and *Howe* for Operation 'Husky', the Allied invasion of Sicily. Operation 'Gearbox' in June 1943 involved a sweep by *Duke of York* and *Anson*, in company with the US battleships *Alabama* and *South Dakota*, to provide distant cover for minor operations in Spitzbergen and the Kola Inlet, while the following month diversionary operations ('Camera' and 'Governor') off Norway were carried out in order to draw the attention of the Germans away from 'Husky'. Before the year was out, *Duke of York* would enjoy her finest hour, and a spectacular victory.

Scharnhorst at Bay

On Christmas Day 1943 the German battleship *Scharnhorst*, in company with five destroyers, made a sortie from her anchorage in Altenfjord to intercept convoy JW.55B. The following morning she was detected by a British cruiser force and engaged on two occasions, during one of which the German radar was severely damaged by an 8in shell. Breaking off and turning to the north in a fresh attempt to locate the convoy, she ran into the cruiser force once more, and in an attempt to disengage came within range of Force 2, comprising *Duke of York*, the light cruiser *Jamaica* and the destroyers *Savage*, *Scorpion*, *Saumarez* and *Stord*. Thus began the Battle of the North Cape.

Duke of York opened with a full broadside, and, in an astonishing demonstration of accurate shooting, aided by radar ranging, two of the ten 14in shells struck home, demolishing the machinery for 'Anton' turret. Gradually the German ship drew away, exchanging fire with *Duke of York*. As hope of catching *Scharnhorst* faded, the four destroyers of Force 2 crept up on her and in a classic pincer tactic fired a total of 28 torpedoes, three of which struck home. Her speed fell off dramatically, enabling *Duke of York* and *Jamaica*, soon joined from the north by *Belfast* and *Norfolk*, to pour a devastating fire upon the hapless German. Further shells and torpedoes hastened the end, and *Scharnhorst* sank at 1945 on Boxing Day 1943 after

Duke of York in April 1943. The decks and turret tops are dark-painted, presumably as a camouflage measure; however, the one feature of a ship under way that cannot be disguised is its wake.

a running action lasting 10½ hours from the first positive sighting. She took with her over 1,700 men.

The Work Continues
Duke of York continued her work in northern waters. In March/April 1944, in company with *Anson*, she was called upon to help provide cover for a carrier strike against *Tirpitz* (Operation 'Tungsten'). Another raid ('Mascot') was launched in July that year and yet another in August: on both operations *Duke of York* accompanied the carrier fleet, but neither achieved the desired result owing to thick fog and the smokescreens laid by the Germans.

The ship paid off for refit in September 1944, much of the work being directed towards equipping her for service with the BPF.

Finale
Duke of York sailed from Scapa Flow on 25 April 1945, accompanied by her sister-ship *Anson*, but a problem in Malta with the electrical circuitry delayed her and *Anson* pressed on without her. She reached Sydney on 29 July, too late to take any meaningful part in hostilities; in fact, she joined up with the BPF on 16 August, the day following the cessation of hostilities. She was present with *King George V* in Sagami Bay for the surrender ceremonies. The following month she sailed for Hong Kong, to be present at the formal Japanese surrender of the colony.

Duke of York remained in Pacific waters until 11 June 1946, when she departed for Plymouth, arriving there exactly one month later. Like her sisters, she was cocooned for several years during the 1950s before being condemned to scrapping in 1957, dismantling being carried out by Shipbreaking Industries at Faslane.

ANSON

Owing to the demands on shipbuilding resources—particularly the need to replace merchantmen and build escort vessels to maximise their chances of survival—the completion of the last two ships of the class, *Anson* and *Howe*, was deliberately delayed. *Anson* was completed in June 1942 and by September was on duty providing distant cover for the Russian convoys. Virtually her entire wartime career would be spent in Arctic and Norwegian waters, frequently in the company of her sister-ship *Duke of York*.

In July 1943 she took part in the diversionary moves designed to draw attention away from the preparations for Operation 'Husky', and in October that year, with *Duke of York* and the US cruiser *Tuscaloosa*, provided cover for Operation 'Leader', in which the US carrier *Ranger* mounted air strikes against German shipping off Norway. In February 1944, in company with the French battleship *Richelieu* and a force of cruisers and destroyers, she stood by in the same capacity while aircraft from *Furious* carried out air strikes against German targets in Norway during Operation 'Bayleaf', and on 3 April she provided cover for Operation 'Tungsten', a successful air strike against the battleship *Tirpitz* (a follow-up raid later that month, 'Planet', and a third on 12 May, failed because of poor weather).

In the Far East
Anson was decommissioned for refit in June 1944 and did not return to the fleet until March the following year, when, in company with *Duke of York*, she set off to join the BPF. By the time she arrived in theatre, hostilities were all but over. She left Sydney on 15 August for Hong Kong, where, together with *Duke of York*, she provided a focus for the Japanese surrender ceremonies. Some of her company were put ashore to help mop up the last Japanese resistance and reinstate public services.

Anson arrived back in home waters on 29 July 1946, and after a short refit was returned to peacetime duties. Like her sister-ships, she was placed in reserve and 'mothballed', spending eight years in this condition before being consigned to the breakers in 1957.

HOWE

Howe joined the Home Fleet on 30 August 1942, her building time extended owing to more urgent demands on the industry. Like her sister-ship *Anson*, she was destined to spend virtually her entire combat career in Arctic waters, covering Russian convoys and acting as a deterrent to any possible break-out by German heavy ships from their lairs in the fjords.

In May 1943, however, she was moved to Gibraltar with *King George V* to take part in Operation 'Husky', the Allied invasion of Sicily, the two US battleships *Alabama* and *South Dakota* substituting for their absence from the Home Fleet. Trapani naval base and Favignana were shelled by the two British ships during the night of 11/12 July.

Based at Algiers, the pair also offered cover during 'Avalanche' (the Allied landings at Salerno), setting out on 7 September and taking in 'Slapstick' (the airborne landings in Taranto) en route. From the 14th of the month *Howe* and *King George V* escorted the surrendered Italian battleships *Vittorio Veneto* and *Italia* to Alexandria. By the end of October, the pair had returned to Britain, and by the close of the year *Howe* had been placed in dockyard hands for a six-month refit.

Task Force 113/57

On 8 August 1944 *Howe* arrived at Trincomalee in Ceylon to join the Eastern Fleet—the first modern British battleship to be deployed in eastern waters since the loss of *Prince of Wales* in December 1941. She was quickly into action, providing cover for carrier-based air operations against targets in Sumatra. In December she moved to Sydney, whence she sailed to Auckland, New Zealand, for a morale-boosting visit.

In February 1945 *Howe* and *King George V* sailed from Sydney to begin operations in earnest in the Pacific theatre; together with four carriers, five cruisers and fifteen destroyers, they made up Task Force 113.

The first major undertaking for Task Force 113 (now redesignated TF.57) was Operation 'Iceberg'—offshore support for the US landings on Okinawa—and this got under way on 1 April 1945. The force was subjected to sporadic Japanese *kamikaze* attacks, but the two capital ships emerged unscathed from their experience. Their two principal roles were air defence and land bombardment, the latter being carried out very accurately, particularly by *Howe* against anti-aircraft installations on the island of Miyako, half way between Okinawa and Formosa.

By the first week in June *Howe* was back in Sydney, and almost immediately it was decided to send her for refit in Durban. It was here that she saw out the remainder of the war.

She was back at Portsmouth by January 1946 and after some years of peacetime duties was, like her sisters, placed in reserve and 'mothballed'. She survived in this condition, at Devonport, until 1957, when she was condemned to be scrapped, a process that got under way the following year.

↓ The end of the *King George V* class: *Howe* arrives at Inverkeithing for scrapping, June 1958.

Model Products

BATTLESHIPS are by and large the most popular warship modelling subjects, a fact reflected in the catalogues of the major kit manufacturers, and the *King George V*s are very well represented compared with some of the other classes of capital ships which saw action during the Second World War. For the modelmaker, there is the added attraction that the five ships, being latecomers to the Royal Navy's battleship inventory, differed very little from one another in general configuration, which means that, for the kit builder, one ship can very readily be modified to represent another of the class; furthermore, their period of active service was short, and major changes in configuration did not occur.

With the advent of low-run 'aftermarket' accessories, there is nowadays a veritable plethora of options available to the kit modeller concerning the level of detail he or she may wish to add without having to fabricate miniature components from scratch. The truth is that, for a financial consideration, an extremely convincing model can be built by those whose skills or patience may not extend to micro-engineering using basic 'raw' materials.

The scratch-builder is well catered for by way of plans and other reference materials, which accounts, in part, for the popularity of the *King George V*s amongst those who work with resin, wood, metal and other more basic materials. In the pages which follow, a selection of plastic kits representing the class is given consideration (this does not lay claim to be an exhaustive review, nor a highly detailed one), and some of the finest models of the ships, both kit-built and hand-made, are illustrated. Whilst the reader may not necessarily aspire to the very high standards achieved in some of the models depicted, he or she should certainly draw a measure of inspiration from them.

↓ Two models in 1/1250 scale by Navis-Neptun—*King George V* (upper) and *Howe* (lower). Within the limitations imposed by their small scale, these metal models are excellent products, well researched and presented. They are ideal for wargaming but stand scrutiny as display pieces in their own right. *Duke of York* and *Prince of Wales* are also available but not, at the time of writing, *Anson*.

Plastic kits

Revell: *King George V* (1/1200)

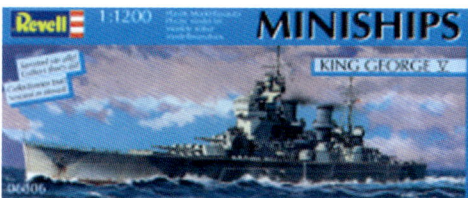

This is a tidy little kit, but one not to be taken too seriously by the scale modelmaker unless drastic surgery is

17

King George V class: Kits and models

	Manufacturer	Scale	Hull	Remarks
King George V	GHR	1/2400	Waterline	Wargaming model
King George V	Navis-Neptun	1/1250	Waterline	Well-detailed model cast in metal
Prince of Wales	Navis-Neptun	1/1250	Waterline	Well-detailed model cast in metal
Duke of York	Navis-Neptun	1/1250	Waterline	Well-detailed model cast in metal
Howe	Navis-Neptun	1/1250	Waterline	Well-detailed model cast in metal
King George V	Eaglewall	1/1200	Waterline	Now rare; long out of production
Prince of Wales	Eaglewall	1/1200	Waterline	Now rare; long out of production
Duke of York	Eaglewall	1/1200	Waterline	Now rare; long out of production
King George V	Revell	1/1200	Waterline	Very basic; ideal for wargamers
Duke of York	Revell	1/1200	Waterline	Very basic: ideal for wargamers
Prince of Wales	Lindberg	1/1000*	Full hull	Inaccurate—curiosity value only
King George V	Tamiya	1/700	Waterline	Depicts ship as with BPF
Prince of Wales	Tamiya	1/700	Waterline	Depicts ship as in late 1941
King George V	Aurora	1/600*	Full hull	Inaccurate—curiosity value only
King George V	Airfix	1/600	Full hull	Depicts ship as in 1940/41
King George V	Heller	1/400	Full hull	Pre-1944 state but AA fit confused
King George V	Tamiya	1/350	Full hull	BPF configuration
Prince of Wales	Tamiya	1/350	Full hull	Late 1941 state

* Approximate scale

performed. The configuration is very generalised (for example, there are six 2pdr mountings, eight 20mm Oerlikon moulded integrally with the superstructure and a single Bofors astern, à la *Prince of Wales*). The 14in gun barrels are pretty grotesque, and a degaussing coil is vaguely described on to the one-piece hull, which also features scuttles moulded a scale two feet proud of the surface. The painting guide is of very little value, showing a disruptive scheme in three shades of grey for the port side only. However, for what it is—a simple kit for youngsters and wargamers—it is worthy enough.

Lindberg: *Prince of Wales* (1/1000)

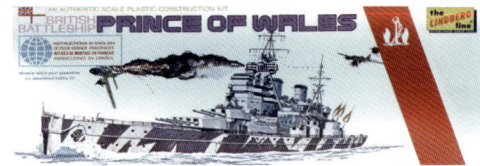

The best that can be said about this kit is that is represents its subject in an approximate fashion, despite the manufacturer's claims that it is 'authentic'. Two extra 5.25in turrets have been moulded on to the after shelter

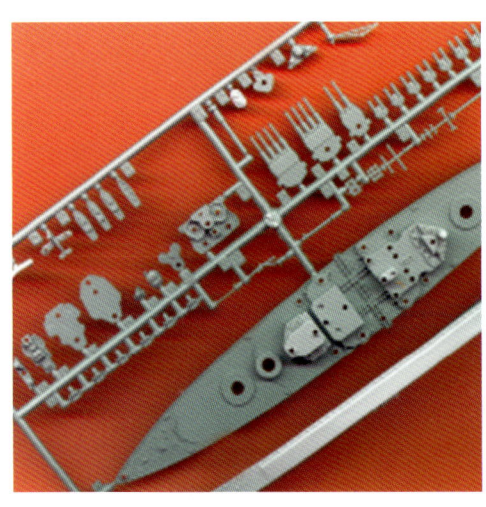
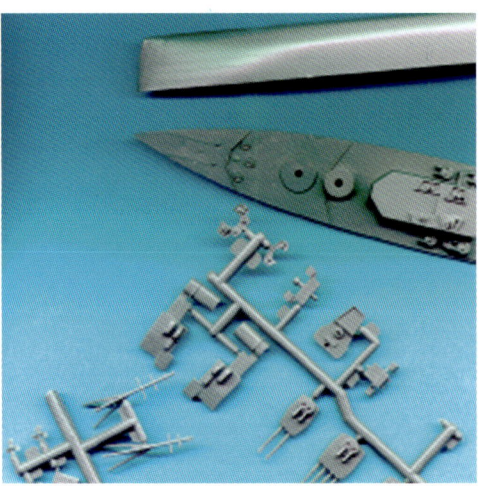

←←Parts for Revell's 1/1200 *King George V* kit—neat and tidy, but very generalised.
←Mouldings from Lindberg's 1/1000 scale HMS *Prince of Wales*. The kit is extremely basic and abounds in inaccuracies.

→→Mouldings for the Tamiya 1/700 scale HMS *King George V*. Despite the fineness of the detail, discretion has been exercised by the manufacturer and the latticework of the ship's cranes is a compromise.

deck, the gun mountings on 'B' and 'Y' turrets appear to be enlarged 5.25in turrets, and some indication of the level of research that has gone into this kit may be gleaned from the fact that the lower hull is equipped with twin rudders and three screws.

Tamiya: *King George V* (1/700)

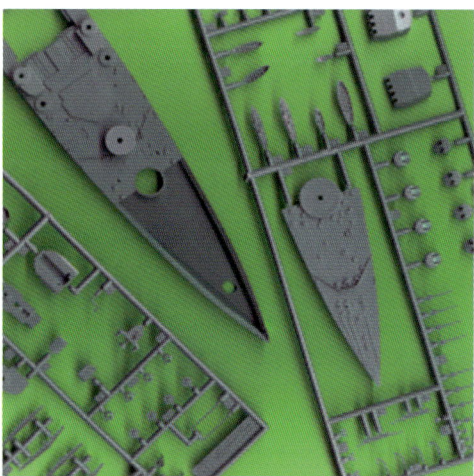

Japanese modelmakers have always shown a keen interest in the Imperial Japanese Navy, and some thirty years ago, in an attempt to tap a hitherto unexplored market, four Japanese kit manufacturers began a collaboration to produce an entirely new style and range of warship kits known as the Waterline Series. They appeared in a scale of 1/700—an odd choice, given that the three scales then in vogue for plastic kits were 1/600 (i.e., 50ft to the inch), 1/720 (60ft to the inch) and 1/1200 (100ft to the inch), the last a popular choice for wargamers who require battlescapes that can be kept within manageable dimensions. They were ground-breaking in another sense too, for they exhibited a level of fine detail never seen before, so much so that for the first time many of the components began to approach something like scale thickness (ever the *bête noire* of the plastic kit manufacturer); moreover, for the first time in the industry, three- and four-way moulds were employed, overcoming that other seemingly insuperable problem afflicting plastic kit technology—the necessity to keep draw angles greater than 90 degrees.

The kits were, generally, well-researched, and not limited to single examples from particular classes. They gained a good reputation; and when some years later, the important subjects from the Imperial Japanese Navy having been covered, it was announced that Allied warships were to receive similar treatment, there was much eager anticipation amongst Western modelmakers.

The two 1/700 kits of the *King George V*s, by Tamiya, did not disappoint: they were generally very accurate, were finely executed, and represented two distinct stages in the evolution of the class. *King George V* depicted the battleship as she appeared for her service with the BPF, with the catapult deleted and with a suitable array of close-range weapons in place; despite the box art, there was no external degaussing cable moulded on to the hull. Bearing in mind the limitations of injection-moulding technology, the kit was, and still is, a remarkable piece of engineering, way ahead of other products portraying the same subject in a comparable scale: vertical surfaces are within an ace of being truly vertical; plating, masts and the smaller gun barrels come much closer to scale thickness than have previous attempts; the 'plank effect' weather decks are restrained; and so on. The kit-builder may be well satisfied: here is a model of *King George V* that looks convincing even straight out of the box, and, for the adventurous, makes a very good starting point for adapting and refining the original.

Tamiya: *Prince of Wales* (1/700)

It hardly needs stating that, in Japan, the best-known British capital ship of the Second World War is HMS *Prince of Wales*, and it is no less surprising that Tamiya's mouldings build into a model of the ship as she appeared when deployed to the Far East. Two of the moulded frames duplicate those on the *King George V* kit, but the third provides, amongst other different components, a revised after shelter deck, an insert for the upper deck amidships showing the athwartships aircraft catapult, a miniature Walrus amphibian and, in an ironic touch, a 1/700 scale G4M1 'Betty'—though quite how this last is to be displayed is perplexing, unless it be depicted in a diorama as one of the two aircraft of the type that was shot down during the final action.

There are no kits of the other three sister-ships of the class in 1/700 scale, but such is the commonality amongst the ships that a *Duke of York*, *Anson* or *Howe* can very readily be produced using the Tamiya kits as a basis. This, together with the popularity of these particular battleships as model subjects, has prompted some of the specialised manufacturers to release accessory kits to aid the builder, and it requires only average skills to build a model of any one of the five, at any stage in her career.

Airfix: *King George V* (1/600)

Although the output of this plastic kit company is nowhere nearly as prolific as it was in the late 1950s, 1960s and 1970s—at least, in terms of new subject matter—most of its warship kits get re-released from time to time. The *King George V* kit is one of the most recent, even though it first appeared many years ago. It is, by general consensus, the most convincing warship kit produced by the company, with the possible exception of the excellent *Repulse* kit.

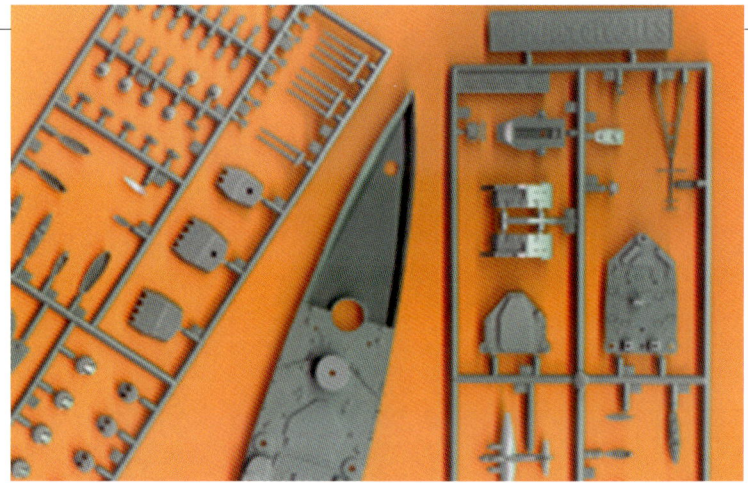

It represents the ship as completed, resplendent in her 1940 dazzle camouflage scheme. The quality of the mouldings is, in places, little short of exquisite, rivalling the best from the Japanese manufacturers; the forecastle breakwaters, for example, are very well shown, and the raised detail on the superstructure mouldings has just about the right emphasis. Airfix have even attempted to demonstrate that the ship's handling cranes are of

↑↑ The mouldings for the Tamiya 1/700 scale *Prince of Wales*.
↑ The Tamiya *Prince of Wales* kit assembled 'straight from the box'. Careful painting helps to disguise the solidly moulded ship's cranes.
↓ Components for Airfix's 1/600 scale *King George V*—one of the best kits this company has produced.

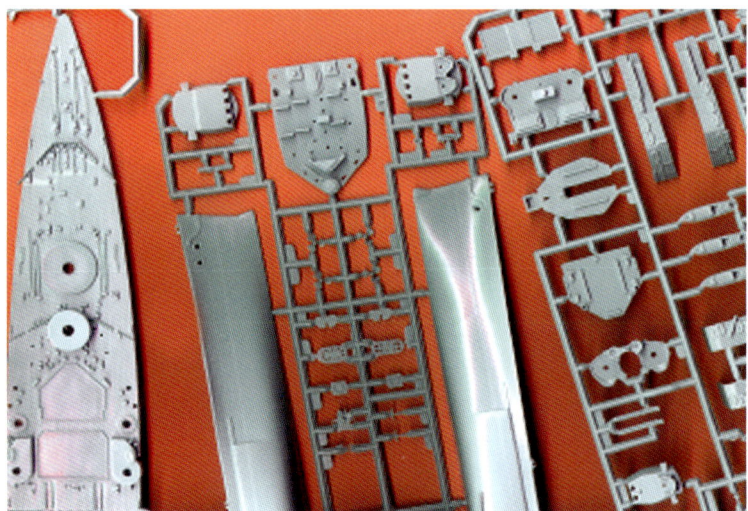

→Scans from Airfix's kit packaging, showing the high degree of realism achieved by the company's designers and toolmakers for a plastic model in this scale.

↓ Revell's *Prince of Wales* does not really 'cut the mustard' when compared with other kits of the *King George V* class ships—nor does it in comparison with other Revell products. Immediately obvious here are the too-high armour belt, the poorly defined moulded anchors and the generally low level of surface detailing.

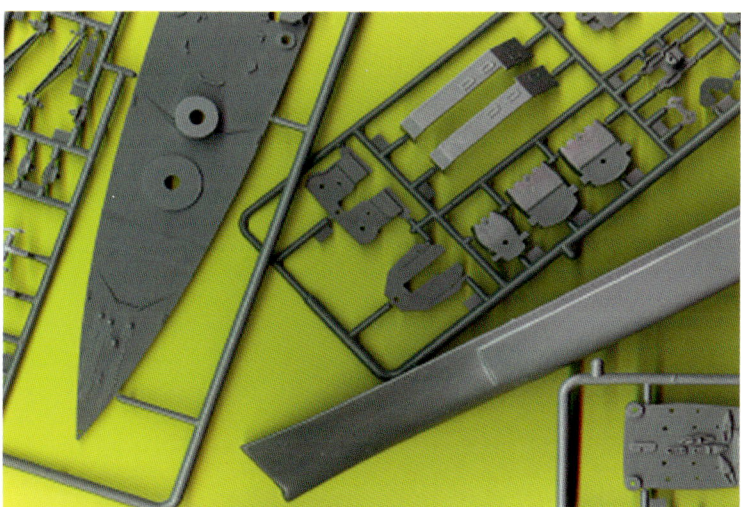

lattice construction and that the funnels have cages across their tops. More to the point, the kit is generally quite accurate in outline and physical dimensions.

One could criticise: there are separate UP mountings for 'B' and 'Y' turrets but the same weapon is represented on the quarterdeck by a shapeless blob of plastic; and the real ship's two-colour camouflage scheme is shown in the none-too-clear painting guide as a three-colour scheme, Airfix having interpreted the heavy weathering on the hull evident on the ship in late 1940 as an integral part of the pattern and, incidentally, eschewing any mention of the contrasting paintwork applied to the ship's turrets and superstructure. But these are trifling matters: this is an excellent offering from one of the world's oldest and best-known plastic kit manufacturers.

Revell: *King George V* (1/570 scale)

The American Revell company is another of the old-established kit manufacturers, and one with a quite prodigious output. The company catalogues have always shown a strong warship content; regrettably perhaps, from the point of view of the model ship builder-cum-collector, Revell seems never to have settled on a common scale (although there are signs that things may be changing in this regard), whilst the quality of its products tends to be somewhat variable.

The *King George V* kit is, unfortunately, pretty mediocre fare. It is reasonably accurate in terms of general appearance, and Revell have got the armament fit and colour scheme right for the first half of 1942 (even if the instruction sheet mixes up the 4- and 8-barrelled 2pdrs), but the detailing is lame, boats and anchors are moulded integrally with larger components, the protective plating is outrageously thick and the catapult track is more in keeping with a model railway layout.

Revell: *Prince of Wales* (1/570)

This kit utilises the same moulds as the foregoing, amended to reflect the differences between the two ships (*Prince of Wales* is shown as in late 1941).

With work, both these kits can be made into models of interest, but a great deal of refining and replacement will be called for in order to impart the necessary delicacy appropriate to the scale. It is good to see that the manufacturer has done some diligent research before producing these kits (and even recognises that there are such things as radar fits), but regrettably the tooling is of a standard that today's modelmakers would find unacceptable.

Heller: *King George V* (1/400 scale)

The French manufacturer Heller has been around since the 1950s and during its early years had a reputation for producing kits of subjects with an indigenous flavour. The range has diversified over the past couple of decades, not least the company's list of warship kits, and a number of British and German vessels have received attention. Thus alongside the names *Jean Bart, Duguay Trouin, Maillé Brézé* and *Surcouf* have now appeared *Bismarck, Scharnhorst, Hood*—and *King George V.* One other unusual facet of Heller's output is that, *voiliers* and kiddy-kits aside, warship kits have almost always been produced to 1/400 scale. The reason is unclear, but no doubt a decision was taken at an early stage in the company's history and there has been little reason to change it. Heller, though, are ploughing a lonely furrow by sticking to this scale.

Apart from the Tamiya 1/350 scale kits (q.v.), this product makes up into the largest injection-moulded plastic model available of its subject class, and it gives a generally convincing portrayal of the ship. Most of the smaller components will require some careful thinning, and the case for some additional surgery immediately presents itself, not least concerning the main gun barrels, the muzzles of which appear to be moulded with large tank-style brakes. There is a gallant attempt at producing the ship's characteristic handling cranes, as there is at moulding a miniature Supermarine Walrus complete with interplane struts. The standard Heller features of brass anchor chain and injection-moulded (and hence outrageously overscale) deck rail are there.

The painting guide depicts the Admiralty Intermediate Disruptive Type camouflage scheme (somewhat removed from the correct pattern) as worn by the ship from mid-1942 (Heller says 1941, in Norway). However, the kit-builder is invited to fit the external degaussing cable around the hull (provided as separate mouldings) and add both UP mountings and 20mm singles (which, most authorities agree, *King George V* never carried at one and the same time).

As a starting point for a showpiece model, Heller's kit is a worthwhile investment, despite its aggravating flaws and a rather contradictory instruction sheet. The moulding frames indicate that a kit of the *Prince of Wales* is or was planned, but to date the hardware has not appeared.

Tamiya: *King George V* (1/350 scale)

In 1984–85 the Japanese 1/700 scale Waterline Series was very well established, Tamiya having gained a reputation for the superb quality of its products in this range. When news emerged that a series of 1/350 scale warship kits was due for imminent release there was much eager anticipation: if the accuracy of the overall rendering and the delicacy of the tooling evident in the company's 1/700 scale products were about to be transferred to 1/350 scale, then modellers were in for a treat.

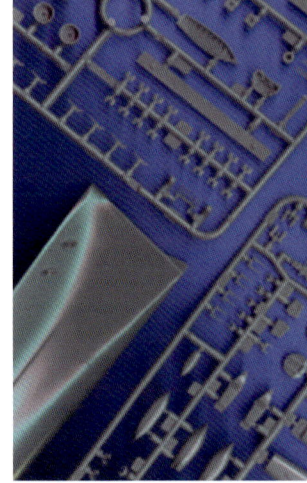

↑ Spreads of parts from the Heller 1/400 scale *King George V* (top), the Tamiya 1/350 scale *King George V* (centre) and the Tamiya 1/350 scale *Prince of Wales* (bottom).

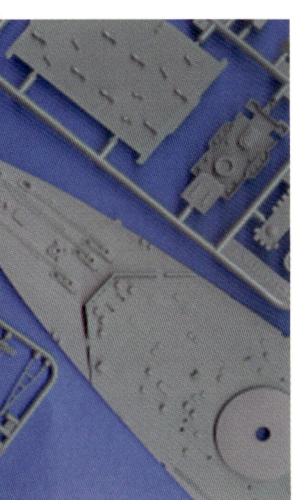
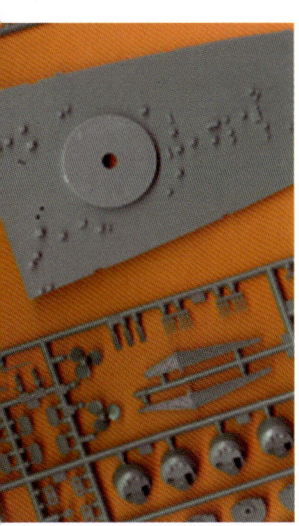

And so it transpired. The two releases again featured *King George V* and *Prince of Wales*, at the same points in their careers as the earlier 1/700 kits, and the components build up into what are arguably the finest and most detailed representations of any warships marketed in the form of pure plastic.

The *King George V* kit has a one-piece hull moulding with propellers, shafts and two-piece rudder as separate mouldings. The forecastle deck is in three portions, the main turrets are four pieces each (barrels grouped together and separate rangefinders) and the 5.25in assemblies are three components each. Draw problems are avoided by providing the major superstructure units with separated screens and decks. Such is the level of detail that the boiler room vents have four (aft) or six (forward) parts each, the 2pdr 'pom-poms' three parts each and the HACS Mk IV three parts each. The masts assemblies are as close to scale thickness as one might reasonably expect.

The philosophy behind the kit seems to have been to engineer what is technically feasible in injection moulding but not to attempt the impossible: therefore the cranes are solid, the funnel cages are solid and there is (fortunately) no deck rail. The instructions are attractive, clear and comprehensive, as is the painting guide. In short, it is difficult to see how this kit could have been improved upon—which is not to say that the detail addict will not want to add his or her own imprint to the model and go much further, substituting and adding tiny components to taste.

Tamiya: *Prince of Wales* (1/350)

This kit utilises essentially the same moulds as the foregoing, amended in generally the same manner as Tamiya's 1/700 waterline kits—i.e. with *King George V*'s boat arrangement and

→Models by Roy Travis built using the 1/350 scale Tamiya kits. Both feature 'after-market' brass-etched parts, but whereas the *King George V* model is otherwise little altered that representing *Duke of York* was modified from the *Prince of Wales* kit. Both depict their subjects in late-war configuration.

additional small-calibre weapons deleted in favour of a suite appropriate to *Prince of Wales* as she appeared during the last weeks of 1941. As before, the Japanese contribution to the ship's sinking is represented in miniature, this time in the form of a G4M1 'Betty' and a G3M2 'Nell'. The third aircraft in the kit, incidentally—the ship's Walrus amphibian—is quite beautiful, comprising no fewer than ten separate parts, including undercarriage and interplane struts.

The painting guide on the side of the box aids the modeller wishing to complete the model as the ship appeared in early 1941; for a few *yen* more, the extra parts needed to build the model in this configuration might have been provided, but they are not included. The camouflage pattern is comprehensively depicted, although caution should be exercised since it deviates in several respects from reality (as, indeed, does the splendid but somewhat freely interpreted box-top painting). Nevertheless, as photographs elsewhere on these pages show, both this kit and its stablemate can be made into stunning display pieces.

Accessory Packs

In many quarters, the legitimacy of a scale model built from a plastic kit is still questioned: forty years ago, such creations were generally seen as 'toys' (and, in truth, some of them looked little better than toys), and viewed askance by 'serious' modellers. This attitude prevails amongst some modelmakers, and there is no denying that a model built from scratch may require skills which exceed those needed to construct a realistic model from a plastic kit. That said, it may be remarked that there are some very inaccurate and poorly built hand-made models in existence!

The Oil Crisis of the 1970s—so it is claimed—together with inflationary trends put an end to the days of the cheap plastic kit, and concurrently sales fell, particularly in the children's market; conversely, carefully researched scale modelling, using kits as a basis, began to grow in popularity, and it was not long before a plethora of small companies began to appear, offering limited-run accessories (and, indeed, complete kits) to meet demand. The warship modeller, traditionally the poor relation because of the high interest in model aircraft, armoured fighting vehicles and other areas, had to wait a while, but before long a number of small companies sprang up, offering exquisitely detailed after-market components enabling small-scale ship models to be produced that rivalled their larger hand-built models in accuracy and delicacy.

White Ensign Models

This British company, based in the West Midlands, has rapidly established itself as one of the leading producers of resin warship kits and photo-etched modelling accessories, and it has an unashamed bias towards Royal Navy subjects. Most of the well-known plastic warship kits—in all scales—are catered for by way of upgrades, and as a result the kit-buyer can pluck virtually any box from the shelf in the model shop in the knowledge that WEM have probably got something in their catalogue which will enhance it.

It is both impractical and pointless to give a run-down of everything that

⬇ The Tamiya 1/700 scale *King George V* detailed with White Ensign Models' photo-etch set and cast resin pom-poms to represent her sister-ship HMS *Howe*. The model is brush-painted using Model Shipways acrylics—accurate in shade but very thick and uncooperative, according to Adam Owens, the builder!

MODEL PRODUCTS

King George V class: Accessories

Manufacturer	Scale	Remarks
Tom's Modelworks	1/700	*King George V, Prince of Wales*
White Ensign Models	1/700	For *King George V* and *Prince of Wales* but allows any ship in class to be built
Gold Medal Models	1/700	*King George V, Prince of Wales*
Eduard	1/700	*King George V*
Tom's Modelworks	1/600	*King George V*
Gold Medal Models	1/600	*King George V*
Tom's Modelworks	1/400	*King George V*
Tom's Modelworks	1/350	*King George V, Prince of Wales*
White Ensign Models	1/350	For *King George V* and *Prince of Wales* but allows any ship in class to be built
Gold Medal Models	1/350	*King George V, Prince of Wales*

In addition to class-specific sets, Tom's Modelworks produce 'general' components—deck rail, light anti-aircraft guns, ladders, crew figures etc—to the scales indicated above and also rail etc in 1/1250 and 1/500 scales; WEM and GMM produce components of this nature in 1/700, 1/600 and 1/350 scales and also deck rail in 1/400 scale; Eduard produces rail in 1/700 and 1/350 scales and naval figures in 1/350 scale; True Details produces etched rail and ladders in 1/700 scale; and L'Arsénal manufactures 20mm Oerlikons and deck rail in 1/350 and in 1/400 scales. The GMM and Dunagain companies also issue decal sheets in 1/700 and 1/350 scales containing such items as flags and pennants.

➡ White Ensign Models produce a vast range of fittings and accessories for the enthusiasts: typical of the range are the 1/700 scale photo-etched set for the *King George V* class, the 1/700 scale 40mm Bofors fittings and the cast resin UP mountings, also in 1/700 scale—all depicted here.

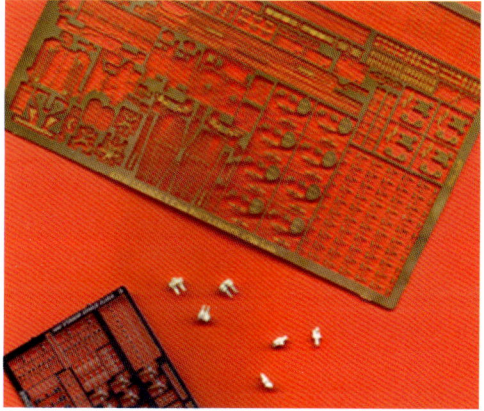

is available from this manufacturer, but a glimpse at one set relevant to the *King George V* class will indicate the sort of 'extras' that the modeller can acquire.

WEM produce etched-metal sets for the class in 1/700, 1/600 and 1/350 scale; as yet there is nothing specifically for the 1/400 Heller kit, although the frame for the Heller *Hood* kit furnishes a great deal that is relevant to the *King George V* class; pleasingly, all three sets provide parts applicable to all five member-ships. Amongst the scores of tiny components provided in these sets, the modeller will find such items as exquisitely defined anti-aircraft gun mounting details, fore- and mainmast components, the handling cranes, boat cradles, very delicate radar aerials, doors and hatches—and deck rail by the foot. The instruction sheet is clear and

➡ Detail from a dockyard diorama featuring HMS *Duke of York* (1/350 scale), complete with crew figures and etched guardrail. The model—the builder of which is unknown—was bought at a sale by Ian Beattie for the princely sum of £25!

25

particularly thorough in approach, with detailed plan views indicating the location of the armament fits and a plethora of scrap views, annotated with helpful advice, identifying the kit parts to be replaced or modified and showing which new parts go where.

In addition to the class-specific sets, literally dozens of other frets and mouldings of a more general nature are produced by this company, including such items as ladders, walkways and anti-aircraft weapons detailing, available in 1/700 (also appropriate for 1/720 of course), 1/600 and 1/350, while in 1/400 there is a set for deck rail and ladders. The range of products is always being expanded.

White Ensign also market a range of 'Professional' cast resin detailing and upgrade components. Again, there is a big catalogue, but components relevant to the *King George V*s include such items as quadruple and eight-barrelled 2pdr mountings, Type 271 radar 'lanterns', a host of miniature deck fittings, all sorts of ship's boats and even 5.25in gun mountings in 1/700 scale; and 'pom-poms' and ship's boats in 1/600 scale. The range of resin accessories in 1/350 scale is at present limited, but it includes a set of five UP launchers.

Gold Medal Models

This well-established American company is another with a substantial catalogue, covering mostly US subjects

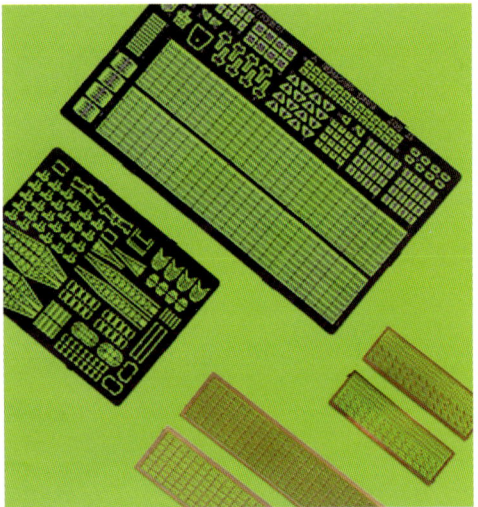

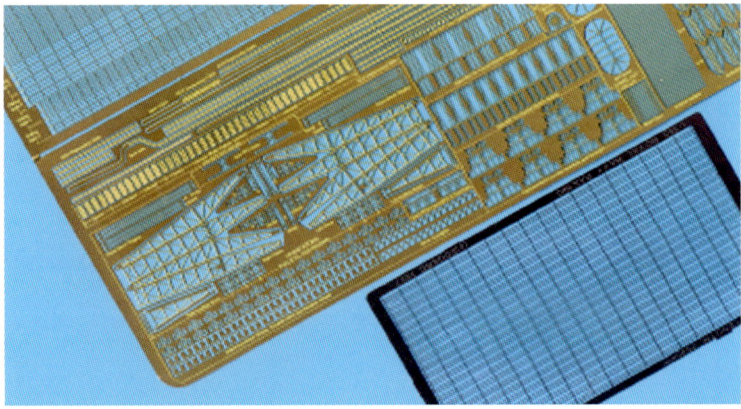

of course but catering also for models of 'foreign' ships as injection-moulded or resin kits are available. As in the WEM set, the etchings produced for use with Tamiya's *King George V* and *Prince of Wales* have direct relevance to the other three ships in the class.

Taking the 1/350 fret as a sample, the quality of the etchings is excellent and the sheet provides a feast of finely rendered fittings. Especially worthy of note are the superb handling cranes and the interplane struts for the Walrus, complete with rigging (but incomplete inasmuch as the inner strutwork is not there); and there are even sets of propellers for the Japanese 'Betty' and 'Nell' aircraft provided in the *Prince of Wales* kit. Much of the brasswork is devoted to enhancing the anti-aircraft gun mountings with such items as protective plating and sights; radar aerials; mastwork and of course guardrail, but oars for the ships' cutters are there also, along with funnel cages and, for the name-ship of the class, the encircling degaussing coil.

The notes state that the fret enables the modeller to build any of the five ships of the class, which is true only up to a point because the radar suite is not quite all-embracing: for example, there are no Type 281 radar aerials, which were distinctive to *Duke of York, Anson* and *Howe.* The instruction sheet sidesteps any comprehensive discussion of the fitting of all the parts, referring purchasers to other reference books, owing to the 'variety in the apperarance of these ships'. Well, yes and no: the *King George V*s

↑ 1/350 scale photo-etched sets for the *King George V* class from Gold Medal Models (upper) and for Royal Navy rail from Eduard (lower).

←←Accessory sets for the *King George V*s from Eduard (top), and brass-etched rail and laddering (two- and three-rail options) from True Details, all in 1/700 scale.

Photo-etched sets for *King George V* and *Prince of Wales* from Tom's Modelworks in 1/350 (left), 1/400 and 1/700 scales.

❗ The advent of photo-etched parts has revolutionised the attitudes of modellers, and these photographs—showing stages in the building of Len Roberto's 1/350 scale *Prince of Wales*—dramatically demonstrate what these details can achieve.

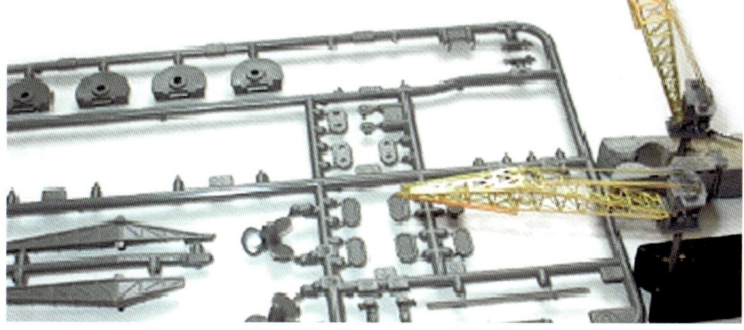

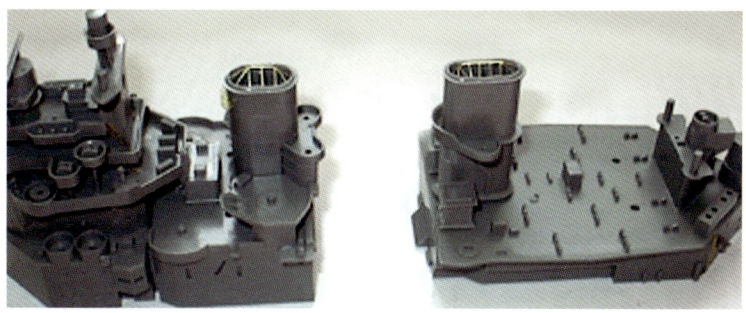

were surely one of the most homogeneous classes to see service. Moreover, while many modelmakers will have the reference books needed to assist them in identifying and locating these detailed parts, the research required to produce them could surely have enabled Gold Medal Models to go into a little more detail with the written word than they chose to do.

Tom's Modelworks

Based in California, Tom's Modelworks offers a very wide selection of ship fittings in etched brass, both specific to the *King George V* class and general in nature. Unusually, the company offers etched frets in 1/1250 scale: and, although this range is generally confined to US subjects, guard rail suitable for all types is available. The sets for the *King George V*s, in 1/350, 1/400, 1/600 and 1/700 scales, are, in common with those of the other major producers, beautifully detailed and a real credit to their originator.

The 1/350 set—to take a sample—differs from those of the two foregoing manufacturers inasmuch as it appears to be designed exclusively for the Tamiya 1/350 scale kits *as issued*: thus there is no external degaussing cable to help the modelmaker 'retrofit' the *King George V* kit, neither are there components specifically tailored for the other three members of the class. The instruction sheet is a little disappointing because it is somewhat basic. It is also, in one or two respects, misleading: the treads for the inclined ladders (or 'replacement stairs'), for example, should most certainly *not* be folded upwards at 90 degrees as indicated!

A point that might be made with all these ship-specific sets is that the modelmaker should expect to pay as much if not more for the accessory sheet as for the original kit: the volumes of sales enjoyed by the specialised manufacturers is only a fraction of what can be expected by the big international plastic kit companies, production runs are therefore very low in comparison and, as a result, unit costs are that much greater.

Acknowledgement

Acknowledgement is made of the following companies, who kindly provided samples for the purposes of these reviews: Heller SA, White Ensign Models, Tom's Modelworks.

Modelmakers' Showcase

MODELLERS are concerned with illusion—the creation of miniature replicas that as far as possible convince the onlooker that he is viewing real objects. Ship modellers are faced with a particular challenge, however, in that the scales in which they work require them to attend to extraordinary detail: in 1/600 scale, for example, a human figure is only 3mm (an eighth of an inch) high. In the pages that follow, photographs of a selection of high-quality models of ships of the *King George V* class, in various scales, are presented, together with descriptive notes, comments about construction and finishing, etc. Most have been built using a kit as a basis, modified from the original by introducing replacement or additional parts to give improved accuracy and/or scale effect; others have been built entirely by hand. It should be stressed that all are interpretations; but, more importantly, all are splendid examples of the modelmaker's craft.

←1 One source of inspiration for modelmakers may be an official builder's model, although these are not always available, may be far removed from the modelmaker's home and may not necessarily represent the ship as she finally appeared. This magnificent creation—*King George V* in miniature—resides in the National Maritime Museum in Greenwich.

KING GEORGE V and ORIBI Diorama 1/700 scale Chris Drage

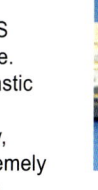

Stages in the construction of Chris Drage's 1/700 scale *King George V*, modified from the original Tamiya plastic kit. Note the delicate 20mm gun 'tubs' in thin grade plastic card, and note also how the painting of the model proceeds as its construction progresses.

This superb diorama utilises the 1/700 scale *King George V* and *Prince of Wales* kits by Tamiya, and also the 1/700 scale 'O' class destroyer kit from the same manufacturer (though originally by Skywave). It depicts *King George V* off the coast of Iceland in early May 1942 just prior to her departure to Liverpool, having recently suffered a collision with the destroyer *Punjabi* (which resulted in the loss of the latter). Alongside in the diorama is HMS *Oribi*.

As can be seen in the accompanying photographs, a great deal of additional work was undertaken, refining, modifying, detailing and, in some instances, replacing the kit mouldings. The kit hull has the degaussing cable added, and the bow damage arising from the collision has been accurately depicted. The 20mm anti-aircraft gun positions on the quarterdeck, after shelter deck and bridge superstructure were built using thin grade plastic card in order to improve scale effect. Ammunition lockers have also been added.

A variety of White Ensign Models etched-brass and resin components were used, both to add fine detail to the model and to overcome the limitations of the injection-moulding process—guardrail, handling cranes, etc. Notice also, in the photographs, the superbly detailed Walrus amphibian, the skilfully painted ship's boats and the particularly delicate rigging filaments.

The 'sea' base was constructed on a baseboard using a combination of plaster and baking foil, sprayed with zinc primer prior to being finished in an appropriate blue.

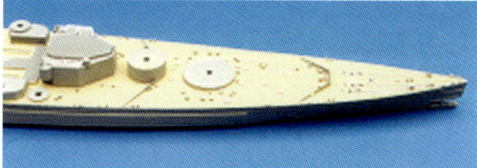
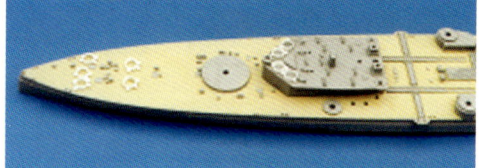
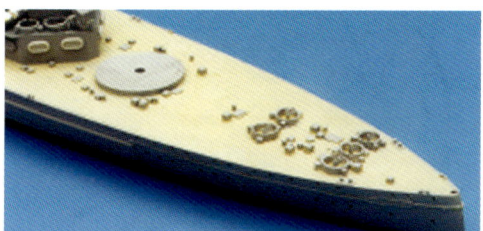
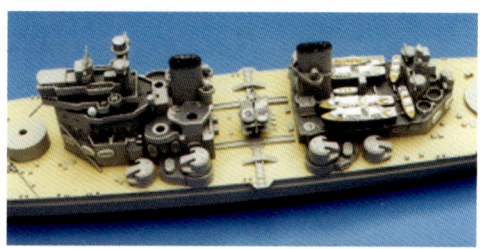

The completed diorama, with HMS *Oribi* in attendance. Deck fittings in plastic kits are generally moulded integrally, calling for an extremely steady hand when painting.

↑ A closer view of Chris Drage's diorama. The battleship's two handling cranes are deployed, and a brass-etched accommodation ladder can be seen along the starboard side—little touches which add to the overall realism of the scene.

PRINCE OF WALES 1/350 scale Patrick Roach

From the modelmaker's point of view, the *King George V* class offers considerable flexibility: with varying degress of effort, any of the five ships can be represented using any of the kits of the class that may be available.

Pat Roach 'backdated' the Tamiya *Prince of Wales* kit to show her appearance at the time of the *Bismarck* episode: broadly, this involved removing the 2pdrs from the main turrets and substituting UP launchers (using resin parts by Iron Shipwright, with the plating made from sheet brass); modifying the 20mm suite; and deleting the Type 271 radar 'lantern' at the foretop and adding the UP director in its place.

Proprietary photo-etchings were added in the form of handling cranes, guardrail etc, and the rigging and delicate mast details were fabricated from 0.005in and 0.008in gauge wire. The model, of course, carries the overall grey scheme typical of capital ships of the Home Fleet at that time.

←HMS *Prince of Wales* by Pat Roach—in 1/350 scale and representing the ship as she appeared in May 1941. Among the awards won by this model has been 1st Place at the 2001 Northern Illinois Modelers' Open (NIMO 8).

↑ Another view of Pat Roach's *Prince of Wales*.

↓ Peter Hall's model of *Prince of Wales*, converted from the Airfix kit of *King George V* and reduced to waterline configuration.

PRINCE OF WALES 1/600 scale Peter Hall

Peter Hall, well known for his work as designer for White Ensign Models, worked on the Airfix kit of *King George V* to produce this fine representation of *Prince of Wales* in the First Admiralty Disruptive type camouflage scheme which the ship wore from July 1941 until the time of her loss.

The model is fully detailed with WEM accessories and depicts the ship in action, preparatory to salvo-firing, with the main armament elevated at differing angles (standard Royal Navy practice for rangefinding purposes). A convincing seascape completes an extremely attractive item.

PRINCE OF WALES 1/350 scale Andy Elwood

Tamiya's 1/350 scale *Prince of Wales* kit offers a first-class basis upon which the modeller can exercise his or her skills in fine detailing—as Andy Elwood's excellent model demonstrates. The five-colour camouflage pattern sported by the ship in the second half of 1941 offers a challenge of a different sort: here, the individual colours were mixed to conform with

The sea base for Andy Elwood's model was prepared using Celluclay and Liquitex gel, painted with manganese blue, cyan and titanium white and topped off with floor polish.

Enhancements to the model include etchings from the Gold Medal Models *King George V/ Prince of Wales* set. GMM naval figures are also in evidence, adding 'life' to the scene.

Snyder & Short colour chips (Royal Navy Sets 1 and 2), using Humbrol enamels and guidance from the camouflage pattern published in *Plastic Ship Modeler*.

The kit is full-hull, so one of the first tasks was to remove the unwanted lower hull. The area of boot topping is lightly detailed on the kit, but cutting through the plastic nevertheless calls for care and patience: applying masking tape around the cut line is one way in which this time-consuming job is made easier.

KING GEORGE V 1/350 scale   Hiroaki Miyai

Here is a different rendering of the Tamiya 1/350 scale *King George V*, with a wealth of detailing by means of photo-etched parts, very intricate rigging and a striking display stand in polished wood. As can be seen from the photographs on this spread, Hiroaki Miyai's standards of construction and finishing are of a very high order.

↑ Weathering effects have been applied subtly and realistically.
↓ A view from ahead showing how the addition of figures not only brings 'life' to a model but also creates an immediate impression of the vast dimensions of the real thing—a point often lost on the casual admirer. Note in these views the neatness of the rigging.
→ The weapons and radar suite and the colour scheme are late-war, although the degaussing coil has been added by the modeller in this instance.

MODELMAKERS' SHOWCASE

35

DUKE OF YORK 1/200 scale Yuri Novak

The 1/200 scale model of HMS *Duke of York* illustrated here is entirely hand-made and utilises a fibreglass hull and wooden weatherdecks, with superstructure components, weapons and fittings in a variety of materials, including metals, plastics and leaf brass. It is, moreover, radio-controlled.

The exquisite workmanship that has been applied to the model is evident in these photographs, and the skills of the builder have been acknowledged with awards too numerous to list in full but including Gold Medals at three successive European Championships—in Odessa in 1994, Constanza in 1995 and Backov (1996)—and a Gold Medal at the 1997 World Championships held in St Gallen in Switzerland.

The model was built by Yuri Novak, President of the Neptune Ship Modelling Club, a group encompassing both professional and amateur modelmakers and based in Makeyevka in the Ukraine. Three years in the making, it features an extraordinary depth of detail—note, in particular, the 'pom-pom' mountings, the ship's boats and the ventilators. The colour scheme chosen is that worn by *Duke of York* in 1944-45 (Admiralty Standard Scheme Type B).

One feature unique to *Duke of York* was the extended emergency control platform on the after funnel, and this is clearly evident in these photographs—as is the vast increase in anti-aircraft armament that characterised all four surviving ships during the last months of the Second World War.

← Two more models of *Duke of York* in British Pacific Fleet configuration from the Neptune club of Makeyevka, these being somewhat simpler (if that is the right word) in interpretation compared with Yuri Novak's model depicted on the previous spread—notice, for example, the detailing on the upper bridge and the 2pdr mountings.

↓ The deck planking on these models is particularly realistic, with subtle variations in shade adding to the overall authenticity of the finish. Awning stanchions have been added to the quarterdecks.

DUKE OF YORK 1/200 scale Peter Beisheim

Peter Beisheim's excellent scratchbuilt model of *Duke of York* shows the ship as she appeared in 1943, prior to the big refit which saw, amongst other modifications, the deletion of the aircraft equipment and rearrangement of the ship's boats; it wears the two-tone (dark hull and light superstructure) scheme applicable to the time of the Battle of the North Cape.

A careful study of available ship's plans is imperative in a complex building project such as this, but inevitably some degree of intelligent guesswork will be required since not every tiny detail can be referenced.

↓ The planked decking on Peter Beisheim's model is finished in dark grey, as are horizontal surfaces such as turret tops and the roof of the upper bridge; note the contrasts presented by the weather decks, which show the 'wear' that would be expected during wartime.

↓ Each of the ship's fast motorboats was created from a block of wood, roughly fashioned and then sawn through longitudinally. The halves were then then 'excavated', joined and given a 'lid' of plastic card, after which the superstructure was built up. The 'glazing' was produced using Kristal Kleer. The handling cranes and Walrus aircraft are totally scratchbuilt.

Schemes

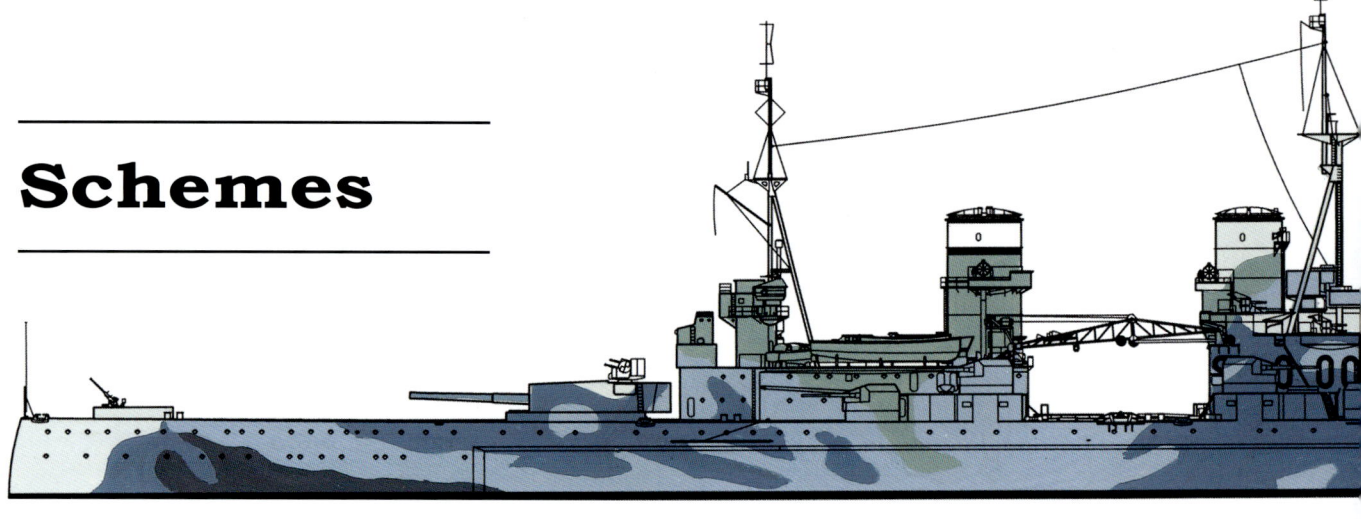

	AP507C
	B6
	MS2
	B5
	MS1

	AP507C
	MS2
	B5
	MS1

PRINCE OF WALES — First Admiralty Disruptive type camouflage, October 1941

Note the white top, trimmed with a black band, to the after funnel—conceivably a device to encourage observers to confuse the ship with her companion *Repulse* during the pair's Far East deployment.

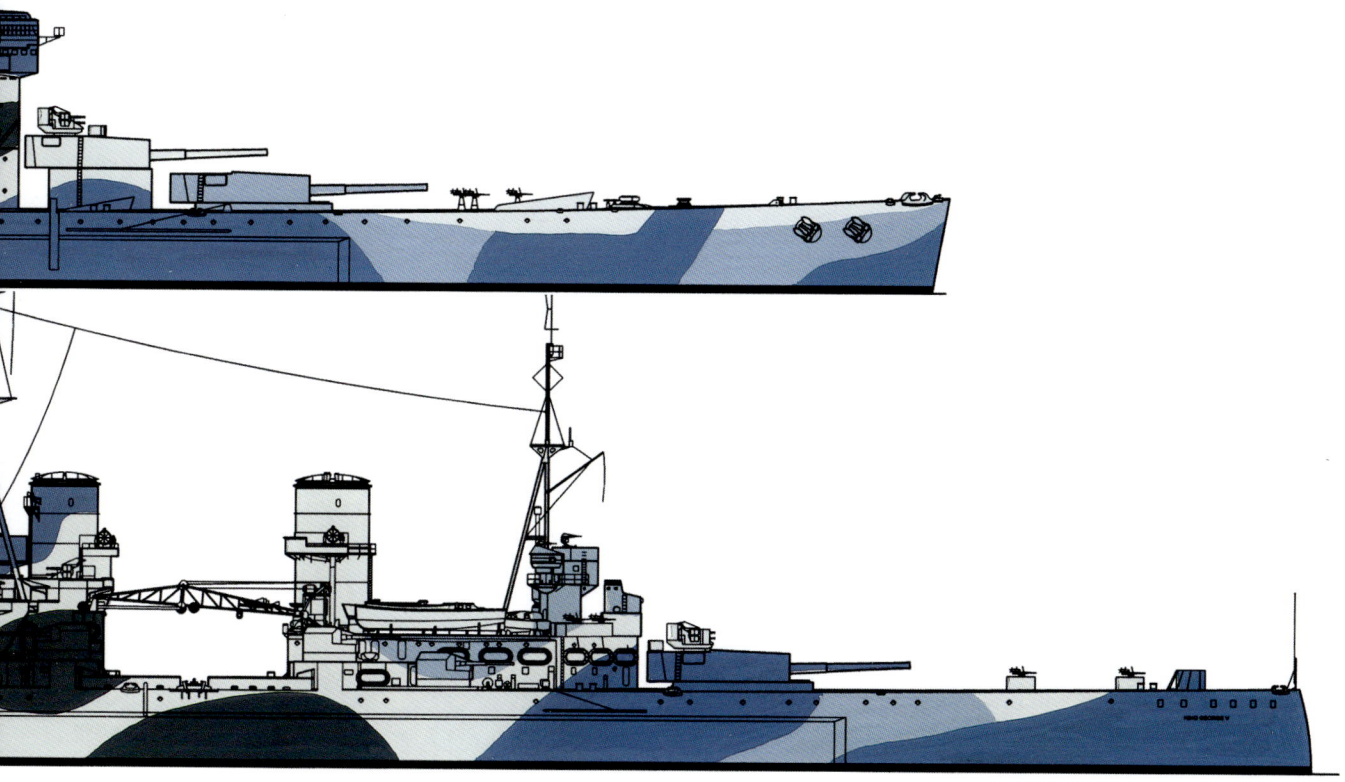

KING GEORGE V — Admiralty Intermediate Disruptive type camouflage, 1943

PRINCE OF WALES 1/350 scale Ian Ruscoe

Here is Tamiya's 1/350 scale kit of *Prince of Wales* assembled, detailed, painted and displayed in a different fashion—a diorama depicting the battleship in the process of mooring at the West Wall, Singapore Naval Base, on 2 December 1941, on her arrival from Colombo, Ceylon, and therefore just eight days prior to her loss. The ship model has been reduced to waterline configuration and set on a sea base incorporating the quay (visible in the foreground in the main photograph), the latter featuring mooring gear and dockyard personnel.

The diorama is in the possession of Ian Beattie, who also supplied these photographs.

The model has a complete suite of photo-etched accessories, including guardrail, ladders, radar aerials, deck fittings and AA gun detailing, all from the White Ensign Models catalogue. A battle ensign flies from the mainmast gaff.

The severe chipping, staining and general weathering inflicted on the ship's paintwork during her voyage across the Indian Ocean is convincingly portrayed.

MODELMAKER'S SHOWCASE

Great attention to detail, in both construction and painting, has resulted in a truly outstanding model.

One of the highlights of this superb model is the extraordinary number of crew figures—in tropical dress for the most part—lining the guardrail, standing atop turrets and elsewhere (one is even moving up an accommodation ladder). The figures are from the Gold Medal Models range.

Close reference was made to the series of photographs available of the actual event in the building of the model.

ANSON 1/192 scale Brian King

Brian King needs no introduction to ship modelmakers, his outstanding craftsmanship being well-known to hundreds of 'model shipwrights'. On these pages we display his excellent rendering of HMS *Anson*, built to represent the ship as she appeared in 1946 after the removal of some of the anti-aircraft armament that was installed for her deployment in Far Eastern theatre.

The model, which is scratchbuilt to a scale of 1:192 (1in to 16ft), won a gold medal at the British Model Engineer Exhibition in January 1999 and a silver medal at the Naviga World Championship held in Mons, Belgium, in 2000.

The hull is of jelutong and the superstructure largely of Perspex and custom-made brass etchings. The weather decks were fabricated from scores of individual miniature planks of 1/32in basswood (American lime) laid over a false deck of hardboard; on the ship herself the decking material was Borneo whitewood. The main turrets were machined from Perspex block, Perspex being an ideal material for such work as it is stable, machines easily leaving a good finish, and takes paint well.

A general view of Brian King's 1/192 scale scratchbuilt model of HMS *Anson*.

A view of the ship's boats (with the blue and white 45ft fast motor boat nearest to the camera). The handling cranes were hand-made from etched brass.

'Y' turret (upper photograph), showing the etched gratings in the Carley floats; and a close view of the cable deck (lower), very well crafted and complete with etched chequered rubbing plates under the studded chains.

KING GEORGE V CLASS BATTLESHIPS

Accuracy aside, it is the attention to detail that differentiates a good model from an outstanding one. The mainmast on Brian King's model consists largely of brass etchings, and the tripod foremast is similarly loaded with etched detail, including the dish-shaped Type 277 radar aerial. *Anson* was the only ship of the class fitted with 'pill box' HA/LA Mk VI secondary directors, and these can be seen in this view. The photograph also also shows the funnel cages—brass etchings of course!

Well-made accommodation ladders improve a static model's appearance and are natural candidates for etching. In common with the rest of the model, these components are 100 per cent hand-made.

The 2pdr 'pom-pom' on 'B' turret has carefully prepared guard rail and optical sights, all delicately painted.

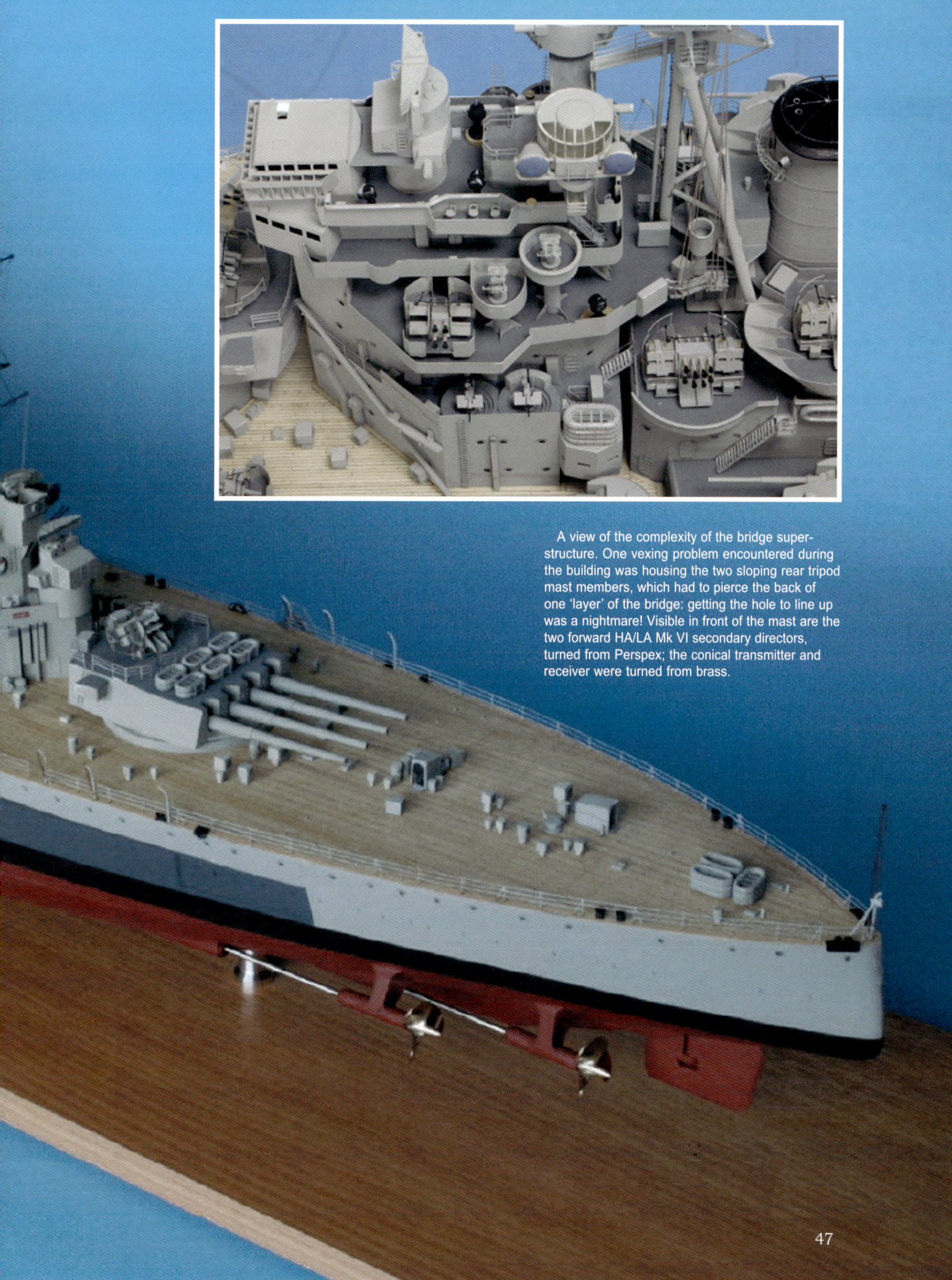

A view of the complexity of the bridge superstructure. One vexing problem encountered during the building was housing the two sloping rear tripod mast members, which had to pierce the back of one 'layer' of the bridge: getting the hole to line up was a nightmare! Visible in front of the mast are the two forward HA/LA Mk VI secondary directors, turned from Perspex; the conical transmitter and receiver were turned from brass.

Appearance

REFITS are *de rigueur* for all warships—necessary in order to re-instil full fighting efficiency by cleaning, servicing, upgrading, replacing and generally improving their systems. They vary in degree and complexity: they may involve just a short stopover in port in order to install some light weapons, or, at the other extreme, they may require very many months in order to effect a complete reconstruction. In time of war, when the ships are worked to their maximum capabilities, refits are naturally more frequent and often, although carried out with urgency, demand that they be *hors de combat* for a considerable period.

War had already broken out by the time the five *King George V* class battleship entered service. Nonetheless, the furious pace at which technology progressed during the years of fighting, coupled with the need to modify vessels in the light of combat experience, meant that they were continually changing in appearance—at least, in detail.

KING GEORGE V

As completed, *King George V* represented the class more or less as it was envisaged at the point of final design (Design 14P). As with the other ships of the class—and typically for warships generally—no reconstruction was carried out, the main and secondary armament remained unchanged throughout her career, and the alterations in external appearance were confined to the area between the

← *King George V* drydocked at Rosyth and almost ready to join the Fleet—one of the series of photographs of the ship taken at Rosyth in October 1940. This illustration offers a good view of the aerials for Type 279 air warning radar system on the main topmast (and carried also on the fore topmast), together with the diamond-shaped FC2 HF/DF aerial lower down.

→ There is a feast of detail for the model-maker in this overhead view, again taken at Rosyth in October 1940. The ship wore an unusual 'dazzle' type camouflage scheme at this time which paid extraordinary attention to detail: even the interior surface of the protective plating around the quarterdeck UP mounting had its outline broken up.

Refit Summary: King George V

Dates	Location	Details
Early 1941		Type 271 radar added
Dec 1941		UP mountings deleted; 1 x 4 2pdr, 1 x 8 2pdr, 18 x 20mm added; UP directors replaced by 'pom-pom' directors; Type 271 radar replaced by Type 273; 5 x Type 282 radars added
May–Jun 1942	Liverpool	Repairs to collision damage; removal of external degaussing coil and installation of internal coil; 4 x Type 285 radars added; FM2 MF D/F added
End 1943		20 x 20mm added
Feb–Jul 1944	Liverpool	1 x 4 2pdr, 12 x 20mm, Types 273 radar and HF/DF deleted; 3 x 8 2pdr, 6 x 2 20mm, 2 x 4 40mm added; Type 279 radar replaced by Type 279B; Type 284 radar replaced by Type 274; Types 277 and 293, 2 x Type 282 and second Type 285 radar added; RH2 VHF/DF added; aircraft and catapult equipment removed and ship's boats relocated habitability improved
1945		2 x 1 20mm deleted; 2 x 1 40mm added

funnels (when the ship's Supermarine Walrus amphibians, catapult equipment etc were landed and the complement of ship's boats repositioned); the close-range armament and their fire control systems; the radar and communications suites; and the ships' paint schemes.

Upon commissioning, *King George V* was equipped with an external degaussing cable which encircled the hull at the level of the upper edge of the main armour belt, except at the bow, where it was led up towards the weather-deck edge in order to clear the hawseholes. She was the only ship of

↓ 'Y' turret, October 1940.

↑ *King George V* in mid-1941.
↓ *King George V* on 10 July 1942, wearing the camouflage scheme depicted in our colour artwork. Although the sun is behind the camera, it is high in the sky, and it has produced long shadows for the edge of the foredeck and port anchor, creating the illusion of a modified camouflage pattern in that area.

the class to have this feature, although it was subsequently removed and fitted internally.

Her close-range anti-aircraft armament comprised four 2pdr Mk VI eight-barrelled 'pom-poms', one pair abreast the foremast and the other abreast the forefunnel, plus four of the bizarre UP mountings, one on 'B' turret, a pair on 'Y' turret and a singleton on the quarterdeck. The somewhat rudimentary radar outfit consisted of Types 279 (transmitting aerial atop fore topmast, receiver atop main topmast) and 284 (rectangular aerials on top of, and on the forward face of, the main director on the bridge). A diamond-shaped FC2 HF/DF aerial was located halfway up the main topmast. Changes to AA and radar suites that took place during the war are summarised in the accompanying table.

The ship was completed in an unofficial camouflage scheme based on First World War 'dazzle' styles and utilising angular areas of Admiralty Dark Grey over Admiralty Light Grey, the intention being to break up the outline of the ship. By late 1940 this paintwork was appearing extremely weatherbeaten. From late 1940 or early 1941 an overall medium grey was applied, and in June 1942 this was superseded by an Admiralty Intermediate Disruptive scheme consisting of four colours, probably MS1, MS2, B5 and AP507C. For her deployment in the Far East *King George V* wore the Admiralty Standard Scheme Type B—probably B20 with a B55 rectangular hull panel—and just before the end of the war the ship adopted the standard capital ship scheme with AP507B (medium grey) hull and AP507C (light grey) upperworks.

PRINCE OF WALES

Prince of Wales commissioned with virtually the same AA fit, and precisely the same radar suite, with which *King George V* had entered service, but the quarterdeck UP mounting had been replaced by a single 40mm Bofors gun and her degaussing coil was installed internally.

It seems that the ship may originally have carried overall dark grey paintwork (perhaps AP507A), but soon after her commissioning this was changed to AP507B. In July 1941, while under refit, she received a complex First Admiralty Disruptive camouflage pattern believed to consist of AP507C, MS1, MS2, B5 and B6. For her Mediterranean deployment and thereafter, the top of her after funnel was white, the separation being defined by a broad black band. Photographs suggest that the deck planking was left in natural finish.

DUKE OF YORK

By the time the third member of the class commissioned, some twelve months after the lead ship, the need for increased AA defence was beginning to be appreciated and radar technology had advanced to the point where new, improved systems were

↑ *King George V* in December 1948.
↑→ Side view of the notorious UP mounting as fitted to *King George V* and *Prince of Wales* upon completion.
↑→→ A view of the bridge on *Prince of Wales*, with the two adjacent port 'pom-pom' directors (Type 282 radar aerials) evident.
→ *Prince of Wales* in late summer 1941. The white top to the after funnel is not yet in evidence.

Refit Summary: *Prince of Wales*

Dates	Location	Details
May 1941		4 x Type 282 and 4 x Type 285 radars added
Jun–Jul 1941	Rosyth	UP mountings removed; 1 x 8 and 1 x 4 2pdr added; UP directors replaced by 'pom-pom' directors; Type 271 radar added

KING GEORGE V CLASS BATTLESHIPS

available. Thus *Duke of York* was equipped at the start with six 8-barrelled 2pdr 'pom-poms' and six single 20mm Oerlikons, two abreast the bridge, two on the after superstructure and two along the centreline of the quarterdeck. Her radar suite consisted of the new Type 281 air warning and Type 273 surface warning sets, Type 284 and four Type 285 gunnery sets and six Type 282 sets for 'pom-pom' direction. FM2 MF/DF was fitted, its

→ After superstructure, *Prince of Wales*, spring 1941. The port HACS Mk IV is at left.
↓ *Duke of York* on 15 July 1942, while on duty with the Home Fleet. Notice the dark-painted weather decks.

Refit Summary: *Duke of York*

Dates	Location	Details
Apr 1942		8 x 1 20mm added
Dec 1942–Mar 1943	Rosyth	14 x 1 20mm added
Early 1944		2 x 1 20mm deleted; 2 x 2 20mm added
Sep 1944–Apr 1945	Liverpool	2 x 8 2pdr, 6 x 4 2pdr, 2 x 4 40mm, 6 x 2 20mm, 15 x 1 20mm added; Type 273 radar deleted; Type 281 radar replaced by Type 281B, Type 284 replaced by 2 x Type 274; 2 x Types 277, 282 and 293 radars added; RH2 VHF/DF added; aircraft and catapult equipment removed and ship's boats relocated; habitability improved
1946		4 x 4 2pdr, 25 x 1 20mm deleted

← ←An excellent photograph of an eight-barrelled 2pdr 'pom-pom' Mk VI on board *Prince of Wales*.
←One of *Prince of Wales*'s 5.25in turrets, its barrels at high elevation.
↓ Her paintwork battered and scarred, and with battle ensign hoisted, *Duke of York* returns from duty with the BPF.

aerial on the front of the bridge. During the war, AA and radar suites were of course progressively upgraded.

Duke of York was the first ship of the class to be equipped with HA/LA Mk V directors instead of the Mk IV fitted to the first two vessels; *Anson* and *Howe* were similarly fitted.

The ship was completed with a unique (and unofficial) disruptive camouflage scheme believed to consist of AP507A, 507B and 507C, the lighter AP507C being confined to areas of the superstructure. The scheme was short-lived, because by the end of 1941 *Duke of York* had been repainted in overall AP507B.

In March 1943 she emerged from refit with a new scheme of dark grey hull and horizontal surfaces and light grey superstructure. The colours are uncertain, but were probably AP507A and 507C, and it appears that the dark grey paint was applied also to the

Plans

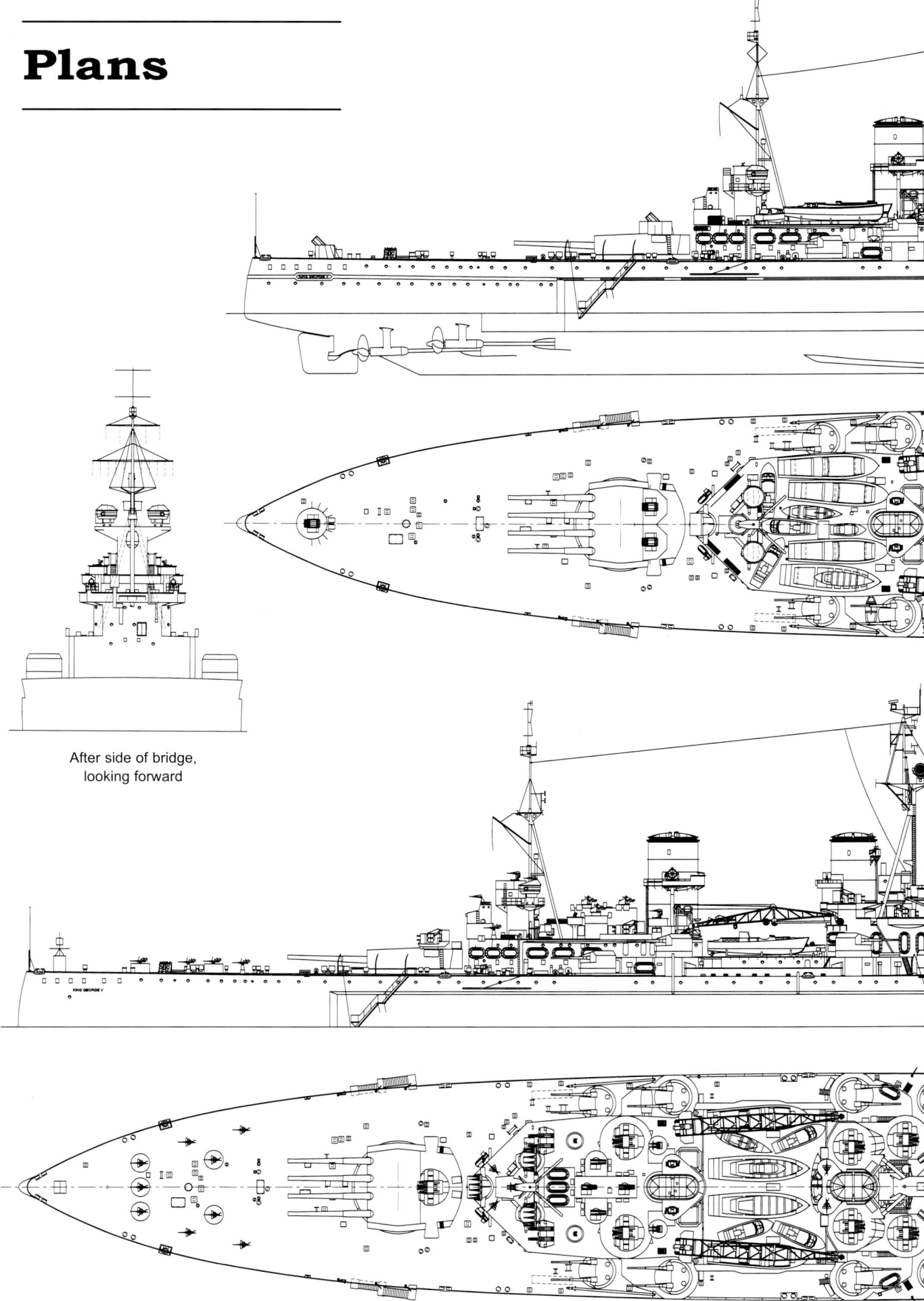

After side of bridge, looking forward

PLANS

King George V 1940

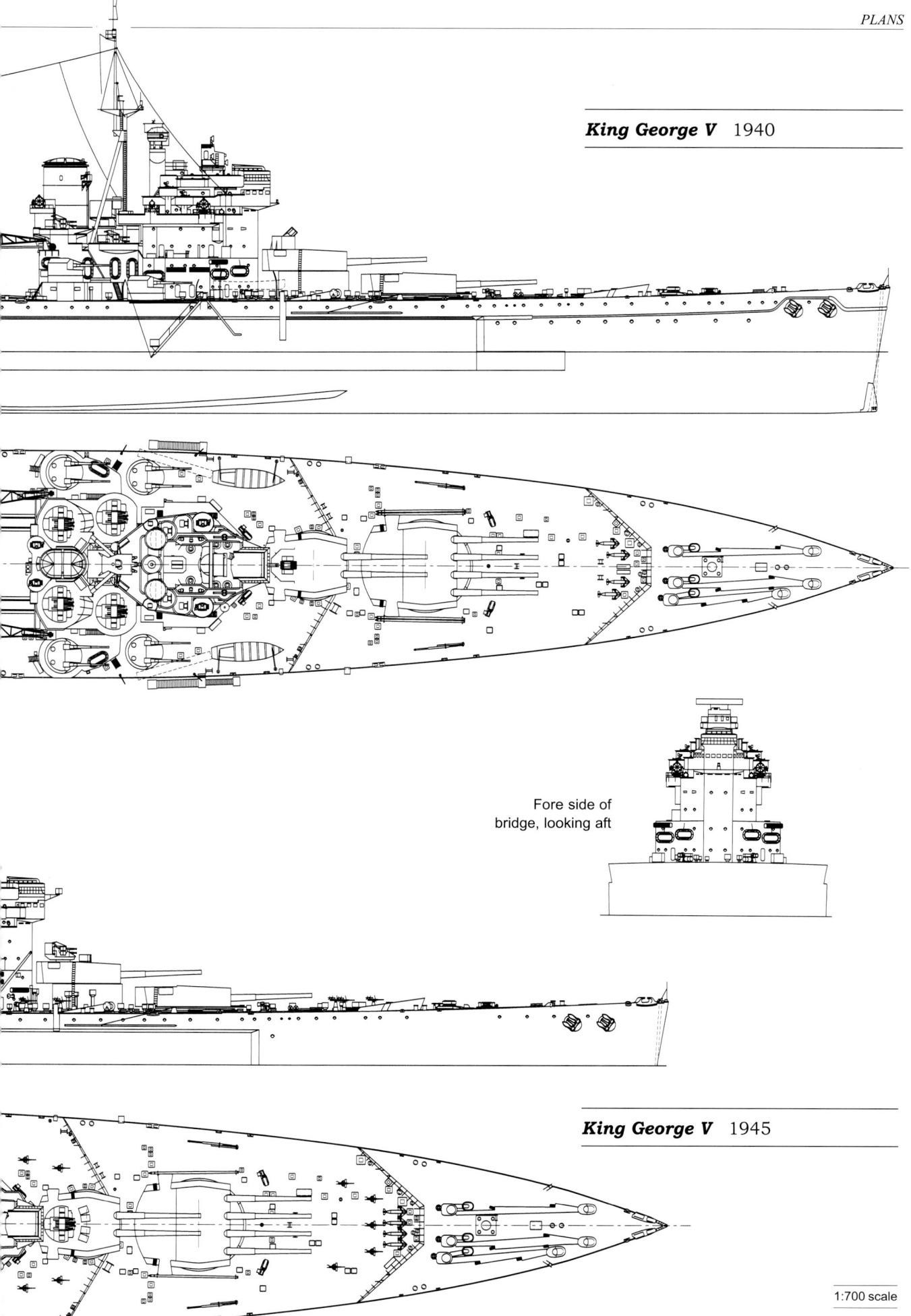

Fore side of bridge, looking aft

King George V 1945

1:700 scale

57

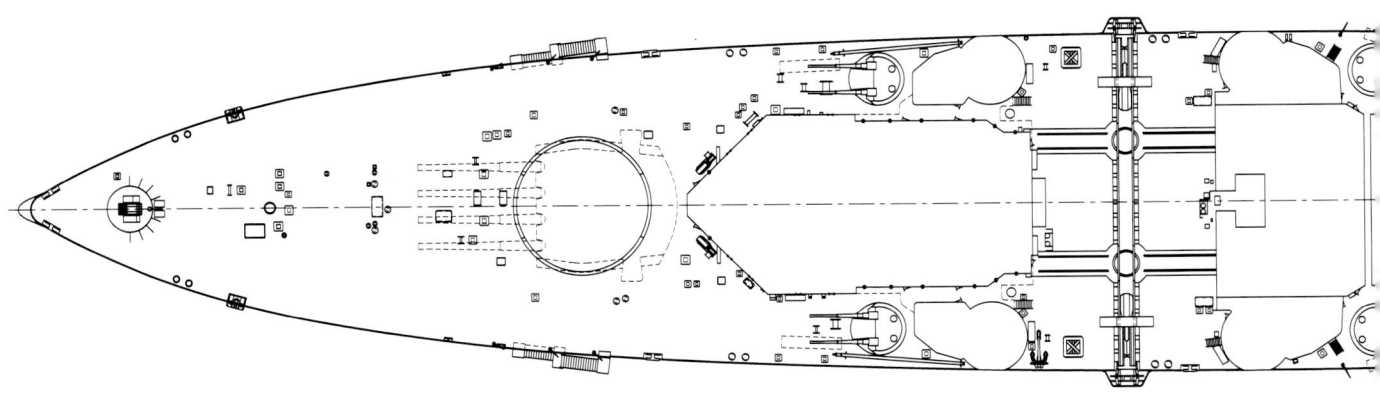

King George V 1940

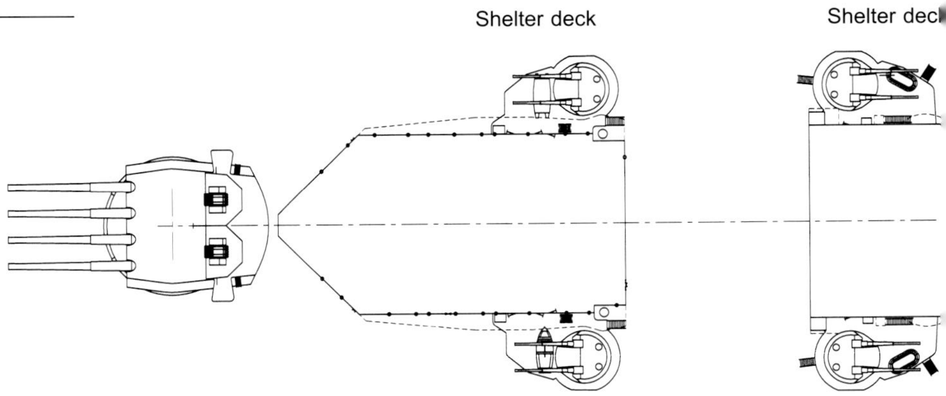

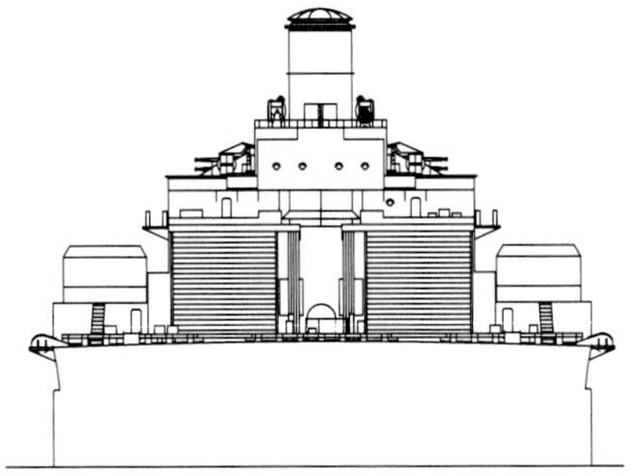

Section at catapult,
looking forward

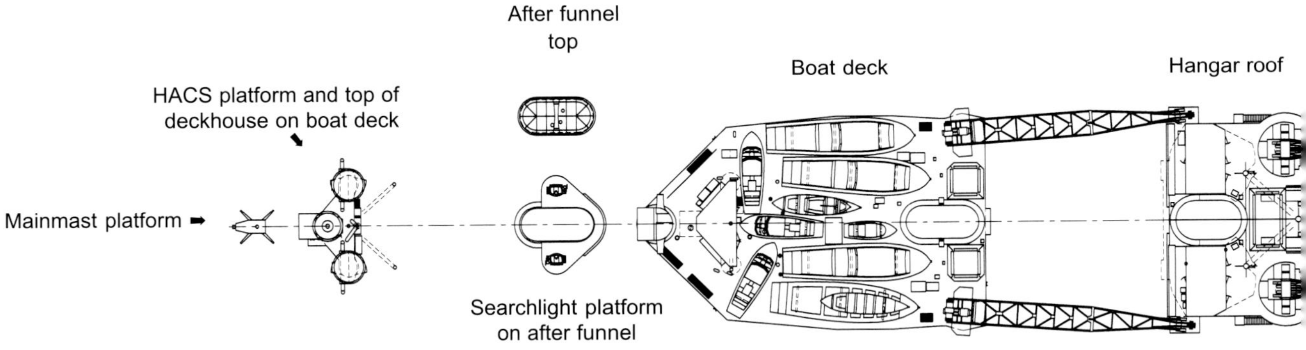

HACS platform and top of
deckhouse on boat deck

Mainmast platform ➡

After funnel
top

Shelter deck

Shelter deck

Boat deck

Hangar roof

Searchlight platform
on after funnel

1:700 scale

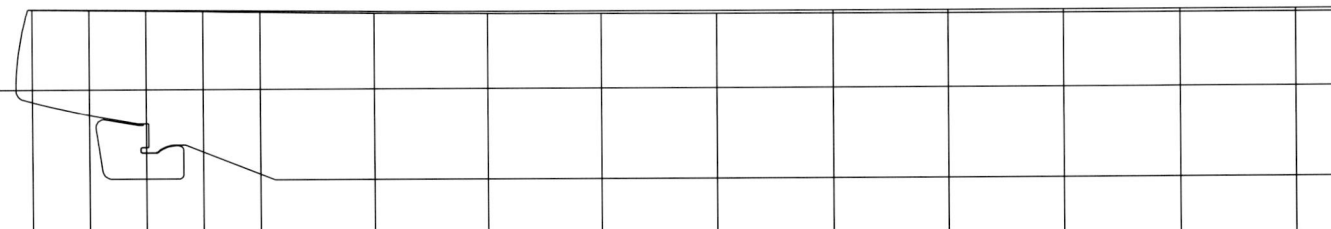

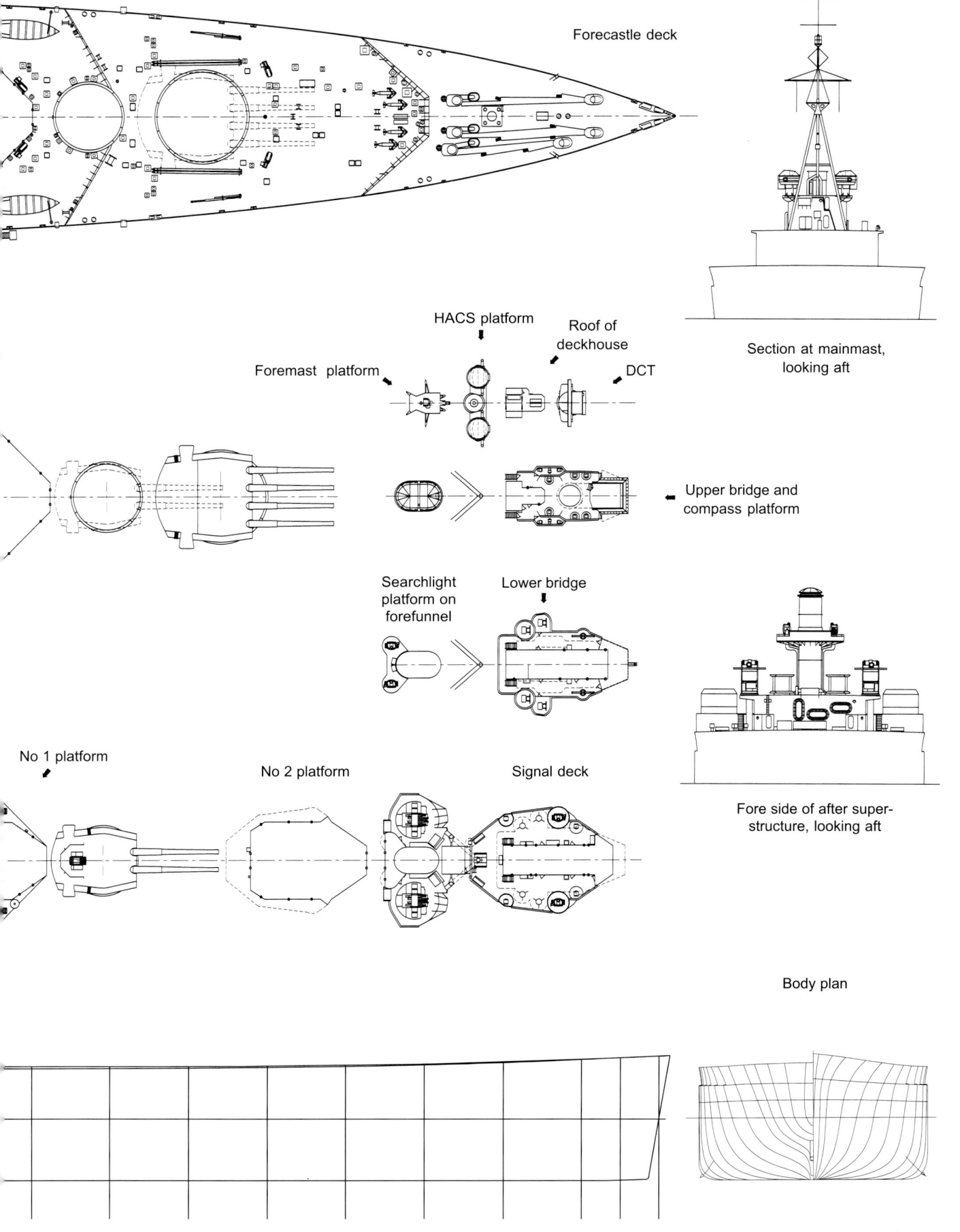

weatherdecks, although the wooden planking forward of the foremost breakwater seems to have been left in natural wood. By the following year the Admiralty Standard Scheme Type B had been applied, in keeping with the ship's duties in the Far East. After the war, the peacetime colours of AP507B medium grey with 507C light grey upperworks were applied.

ANSON

Anson joined the Fleet some seven months after *Duke of York*, and her original AA battery comprised six 8-barrelled 2pdr Mk VI and eighteen 20mm. The radar suite was essentially the same as that of her predecessor in the class. However, in later life *Anson* could be distinguished from the other ships in the class in having a different pattern of secondary HACS fitted, the Mk VI, and Type 651 missile-jamming equipment, with aerials for the latter on mainmast outriggers.

She left her builders wearing an Admiralty Intermediate Disruptive camouflage scheme believed to employ AP507A, AP507B, AP507C and B5. This scheme was in place until her 1944–45 refit, when the usual Admiralty Standard Type B was applied for the ship's service with the British Pacific Fleet. In 1946 she was wearing the postwar dark hull and light upperworks scheme—probably AP507B and

⬇ Damaged foremast, *Duke of York*, following the engagement with *Scharnhorst*.
⬇⬇ *Duke of York* in 1945, in the standard BPF scheme for capital ships.

Refit Summary: Anson		
Dates	Location	Details
Early 1943		22 x 1 20mm added
Jul 1944–Mar 1945	Devonport	2 x 8 2pdr, 4 x 4 2pdr, 2 x 4 40mm, 8 x 2 20mm, 13 x 1 20mm added; Type 273 radar deleted; Type 281 radar replaced by Type 281B, Type 282 replaced by Type 262 and two more Type 262 added, Type 284 replaced by 2 x Type 274, Type 285 replaced by Type 275; Type 277 and 293 added; RH2 VHF/DF, Type 651 jammer added; HA/LA Mk V directors replaced by HA/LA Mk VI; aircraft and catapult equipment removed and ship's boats relocated; habitability improved
Mid 1945		2 x 2 20mm replaced by 2 x 4 2pdr
1946		4 x 2, 2 x 8 2pdr deleted

↓ *Duke of York* in December 1946, bereft of most of her wartime AA armament.

AP507C—and by 1948 she was finished in overall light grey, a scheme she wore until she finally paid off.

HOWE

The last ship of the *King George V* class to be completed, *Howe* joined the Fleet with the the same complement of AA weapons as *Anson* and a similar radar suite to that installed in *Anson* and *Duke of York*. As can be seen from the table, subsequent upgrades set the pattern for the surviving ships of the class.

From the time of her commissioning until early 1945 *Howe* carried an Admiralty Standard Type camouflage pattern very similar (though not identical) to that applied to *Anson*. Photographic evidence shows that at some point during this period she was repainted, at least in part, because the disruptive pattern around the bow and in other areas changed both in colour and in shape. For her Far East deploy-

ment the usual Admiralty Standard Type B was employed, the dark hull panel reaching up to the top of the main armour belt but extending well beyond it forward and to a lesser degree aft. This new paint scheme may well have been applied while the ship was in New Zealand waters: *Howe* was certainly still wearing disruptive camouflage when she first arrived there, yet photographs evidently taken in Auckland show her having discarded it in favour of a hull painted medium grey (probably AP507B) and superstructure, turrets, etc light grey (probably AP507C). By September 1945, however, she had been repainted

↑↑*Anson* in March 1944, at about the time of Operation 'Husky'.
↑ *Anson* in summer 1946, in her postwar two-tone grey scheme. Notice the Type 651 missile-jamming aerials—unique to this ship— mounted on the mainmast tripod struts.
→↑*Howe* at speed, May 1944. As can be seen, the camouflage schemes worn by *Howe* and *Anson* at this time, though nominally the same, were not quite identical in pattern.
→ *Howe* in 1946. The heavy close-range armament that equipped all four surviving ships at the end of the Second World War was quickly dispensed with.

again, in the Admiralty Standard Type B scheme. The following year she reverted to a medium grey hull and light grey upperworks, and from about 1948 she was finished in overall light grey.

APPEARANCE

Refit Summary: *Howe*

Dates	Location	Details
Early 1943		22 x 1 20mm added
Dec 1943–May 1944	Devonport	6 x 1 20mm deleted; 2 x 8 2pdr, 2 x 4 40mm, 4 x 2 20mm added; Type 273 radar deleted; Type 281 radar replaced by Type 281B, Type 282 replaced by Type 262 and two more Type 262 added, Type 284 replaced by Type 274; one more Type 285 added; Type 277 and 293 added; RH2 VHF/DF added; aircraft and catapult equipment removed and ship's boats relocated; habitability improved
Jun–Sep 1945	Durban	34 (all) x 1 20mm deleted; 6 x 4 2pdr, 18 x 1 40mm added
Late 1945		6 x 1 40mm deleted
21 Jan–14 Mar 1946	Portsmouth	6 x 4 2pdr, 8 x 1 40mm deleted
May 1948–June 1949	Devonport	2 x 4 40mm deleted

Selected References

BOOKS

Beisheim, Peter (ed.), *Building Model Warships of the Iron and Steel Eras*, Chatham Publishing (London, 2002)

Breyer, Siegfried, *Battleships and Battlecruisers, 1905–1970*, Macdonald (London, 1973)

Brown, D. K., *A Century of Naval Construction*, Conway Maritime Press (London, 1983)

—— (ed.), *The Design and Construction of British Warships, 1939–1945* (3 vols), Conway Maritime Press (London, 1995)

——, *Nelson to Vanguard*, Chatham Publishing (London, 2000)

Brown, David, *Warship Losses of World War Two*, Arms and Armour Press (London, 1990)

Campbell, V-Adm Sir Ian, and Macintyre, Capt Donald, *The Kola Run*, Frederick Muller (London, 1958)

Chesneau, Roger (ed.), *Conway's All the World's Fighting Ships, 1922–1946*, Conway Maritime Press (London, 1980)

Coward, Cdr B. R., *Battleships at War*, Ian Allan (Shepperton, 1987)

Friedman, Norman, *Battleship Design and Development, 1905–1945*, Conway Maritime Press (London, 1978)

Hodges, Peter, *The Big Gun*, Conway Maritime Press (London, 1981)

Hough, Richard, *The Hunting of Force Z*, Collins (London, 1963)

Kennedy, Ludovic, *Pursuit: The Sinking of the Bismarck*, Collins (London, 1974)

Middlebrook, M., and Mahoney, P., *Battleship: The Loss of the Prince of Wales and Repulse*, Allen Lane (London, 1977)

Parkes, Oscar, *British Battleships*, Seeley Service (London, 1957)

Raven, Alan, and Roberts, John, *British Battleships of World War Two*, Arms and Armour Press (London, 1976)

——, *King George the Fifth Class Battleships* ('Ensign 1'), Bivouac Books (London, 1972)

Roberts, John, *British Warships of the Second World War*, Chatham Publishing (London, 2000)

Roskill, Capt S. W., *The War at Sea* (3 vols), HMSO (London, 1954–61)

Rhys-Jones, Graham, *The Loss of the Bismarck: An Avoidable Disaster*, Cassell & Co (London, 1999)

Rohwer, J., and Hummelchen, G., *Chronology of the War at Sea: The Naval History of World War Two*, Greenhill Books (London, 1992)

Tarrant, V. E., *King George V Class Battleships*, Arms and Armour Press (London, 1991)

Williams, David, *Naval Camouflage 1914–1945*, Chatham Publishing (London, 2001)

Winton, John, *The Death of the Scharnhorst*, Antony Bird (Chichester, 1983)

PLANS

David MacGregor Plans, 12 Upper Oldfield Park, Bath, Avon, BA2 3JZ, England

National Maritime Museum, Greenwich, London SE10 9NF, England

Public Record Office, Kew, Richmond, Surrey TW9 4DU, England

VIDEOS

Naval Videos Time Capsules: *Part 1: Battleships at War 1941/42*

DD Videos: DD2422 *The British Pacific Fleet*

DD Videos: DD2999 *The Scharnhorst, Part 2*

WEBSITES (Specialist)

http://www.forceZ-survivors.org.uk
http://www.geocities.com/hmsdukeofyork

WEBSITES (General/modelling)

http://www.shipcamouflage.com
http://www.internetmodeler.com
http://www.modelwarships.com
http://warship.simplenet.com
http://smmlonline.com